QUEER ICONS

PATRICK BOYLE ILLUSTRATED BY ANTOINE CORBINEAU

QUEER ICONS

FROM GAY TO Z

ARTISTS, ACTIVISTS & TRAILBLAZERS

Smith Street Books

CONTENTS

The Icons ... 10–109

INTRODUCTION

A lot of crazy shit runs through your mind before coming out as queer. My own thoughts from that period of my life were pretty dramatic: *Will my parents still love me? Am I going to have to start from scratch? Where am I supposed to find sequinned hotpants?*

In those moments of panic, the thought that my queerness could be *fun* never crossed my mind. No one's telling closeted school kids that, when they're ready, and if they're so inclined, they have a second family lying in wait. It's a family without borders or limits, replete with some of the weirdest and most wonderful relatives imaginable.

I'm talking about the LGBTQ+ community, of course: a collective united by our shared history in the margins, our experiences of otherness. Here, individuality isn't simply encouraged; it's a prerequisite. We're always accepting new members, growing as we learn more from each and every one of them.

This volume celebrates, in a vaguely alphabetical order (because I failed to find a good icon starting with Z), some of the most iconic figures of our diverse and eclectic community. Read up on fearless activists, key players of the Stonewall Riots, Olympic gold medallists, giants of the music industry, directors and stars of feature films, legends of literature, offbeat comedians, lively drag queens, and those in the public eye who use their platforms to champion visibility. In short: a bunch of queer icons.

As a basic white boy, I was tempted to fill these pages with the likes of Judy Garland, Cher, Kylie Minogue, Lady Gaga and the many allies who are lavishly praised as 'gay icons'. But we're here to talk exclusively about the fam – with the exception of a nod to some of our most recognisable allies on page 26. (To any lovely allies looking for a simple way to support the queer community: have you considered buying a copy of this book for yourself, three friends, five colleagues and all of your neighbours and their pets?)

Now, you might be asking yourself: why waste time peering in the rear-view mirror (or into the fun lives of celebrities) when there are daily reports of atrocities committed against queer people around the world? At the time of writing, Chechnya is reportedly torturing and purging their LGBTQ+ community; homosexuality remains an offence punishable by death in nine countries, including Iran, Saudi Arabia and Qatar; and suicide rates in the queer community remain shockingly high in comparison to the general population, no matter where you are in the world.

While it's true that the queer community is still under fire, it's also true that solidarity and visibility are some of the best forms of defence. By celebrating and raising each other up, we empower everyone in our community. It's for this very reason that I have peppered throughout this queer alphabet some reflections on queer history and timelines of our visibility in certain fields. They're our stories to tell and to remember.

But that's enough from me – let's get to the icons. It's because of trailblazers such as these that a book like this could ever exist. A big, queer thank you to all.

1919: The first queer film, *Different from the Others*, is released in Germany.

1926: *The New York Times* becomes the first major publication to use the term 'homosexuality'.

1933: Along with the Jewish community and other minorities, LGBTQ+ people in Germany are sent to concentration camps, where an estimated 3000–9000 would eventually die.

1938: The film *Bringing Up Baby* becomes the first film to use the term 'gay' to describe homosexuality. (Debatably.)

1954: Lord Montagu – and many other British men from both high and regular society – are convicted for 'consensual homosexual offences'.

1966: The Mattachine Society stages a peaceful 'sip-in' protest at a bar in New York City, opposing a prohibition against serving alcohol to queer men.

1969: The Stonewall Riots (see page 49) mark, for many, the beginning of the modern fight for LGBTQ+ rights in the US and around the world.

1973: The American Psychiatric Association retracts its definition of homosexuality as a mental disorder.

1978: City Supervisor Harvey Milk (see page 64) is murdered at San Francisco City Hall.

1981: The first cases of HIV/AIDS are reported in the US.

1989: Denmark becomes the first country to create registered partnerships for same-sex couples.

1991: The red ribbon is first used a symbol to raise awareness for HIV/AIDS.

1994: Canada grants asylum to LGBTQ+ people fearing persecution in their home countries.

1997: Ellen DeGeneres (see page 20) comes out as a lesbian, changing the landscape of US TV.

1998: Matthew Shepard is brutally murdered in Laramie, Wyoming.

2001: The Netherlands becomes the first country to legalise same-sex marriage.

2009: Jóhanna Sigurðardóttir (see page 90) becomes the Prime Minister of Iceland and the first openly queer leader in history.

2011: The US military's 'Don't ask, don't tell' policy is repealed, ending the ban on queer people serving openly in the armed forces.

2013: The Parliament of the United Kingdom passes the Marriage (Same Sex Couples) Act.

2015: The historically conservative and predominantly Catholic Republic of Ireland becomes the first country to legalise same-sex marriage by popular vote ('Yes' won with a large majority).

2015: The Supreme Court of the United States makes same-sex marriage legal in all fifty states.

2016: The Stonewall National Monument becomes the first designated LGBTQ+ monument in the US.

2016: 41 openly LGBTQ+ athletes compete at the Olympic Games in Rio de Janeiro.

2017: The Australian Marriage Law Postal Survey allows the country to weigh in on same-sex marriage, with a majority in support. One month later, same-sex marriage is legalised.

Pedro Almodóvar

In addition to enjoying a reputation as Spain's most acclaimed filmmaker, Pedro Almodóvar is a bona fide pioneer of queer cinema. In the stylised and colour-saturated worlds of Almodóvar's making, you'll find plenty of complex queer characters: ones who forgo the standard coming-out narrative, who instead endure gritty and perverse struggles. In doing so, these queer characters are spotlighted in each film because of their humanity, rather than their sexuality.

Almodóvar actually rejects his repeated categorisation as an LGBTQ+ filmmaker; he sees his films as intended for all audiences – which, obviously, they are. The awards alone support this: *All About My Mother* (1999) snagged the Academy Award for Best Foreign Language Film, while *Talk to Her* (2002) won the Academy Award for Best Original Screenplay. These films – like all of Almodóvar's most critically and commercially successful work – triumph because of their realistic representation of marginalised characters.

While Almodóvar's work often explores the relationship between gay men and straight women, challenges sexual power dynamics in heterosexual couples, and features gender-bending, what truly makes his films inherently queer is their focus on people on the fringes of society. (Also, they're funny and super-pretty, but that's just a bonus.)

Gilbert Baker

It's thanks largely to American artist Gilbert Baker that celebrations of pride around the world are so damn colourful. Baker designed the rainbow flag in San Francisco in 1978 as a unifying symbol to galvanise the queer-rights movement. Before his rainbow design, the pink triangle was the most recognisable LGBTQ+ symbol, but considering that it was conceived by the Nazis to literally label people suspected of being queer, Baker was probably justified in wanting an overhaul.

The flag's initial design originally featured eight colours, including pink, turquoise and indigo. After the assassination of local politician Harvey Milk (see page 64), demand for rainbow flags skyrocketed; pink fabric was in short supply, so the colour was removed from the design. In 1979, turquoise and indigo were replaced with one strip of royal blue, giving us the six-colour flag we know today.

Baker ensured that the flag's design remained in the public domain, allowing it to be reproduced by anyone. This cleared the way for rainbow swag to be made and sold globally, cementing the flag's status as an enduring symbol of pride. Two years before Baker's death in 2017, New York City's MOMA acquired the original flag for its design collection, recognising and immortalising its cultural and aesthetic value.

Josephine Baker

The famously banana-clad entertainer and activist Josephine Baker was born Freda Josephine McDonald in St Louis, Missouri. Much of Baker's impoverished childhood was spent on that city's streets, where she made a living by dancing on corners. She performed in a number of local vaudeville dance troupes before moving to New York City at the age of fifteen. Baker performed around the US and parts of western Europe before relocating to Paris when she was nineteen.

Paris in 1925 was in the throes of jazz-soaked indulgence. Baker immediately garnered wide recognition there as a gifted performer, wowing audiences with her cheeky eroticism – most famously in her *Danse Sauvage*, for which she sported little more than a skirt made of rubber bananas. By twenty-one she was a sensation around Europe, and developed a successful career in film and music. A true quadruple threat, Baker used her celebrity privileges for good during the Second World War, smuggling messages for the French Resistance. These were often written on her sheet music using invisible ink.

Although Baker was married to four men in her lifetime, she also had affairs with women; French novelist Colette and cultural icon Frida Kahlo (see page 51) were reportedly among them. Baker vehemently denied her bisexuality but remains a queer icon thanks to her resilience and success as an outsider.

James Baldwin

James Baldwin was one of the great literary minds of the twentieth century. In his work as a novelist, playwright, essayist and civil-rights activist, Baldwin drew upon his experience growing up as an African American in New York City in the aftermath of the Great Depression. The hyper-intelligent young man spent his formative years frustrated by the lack of education available to him, and turned his energies to writing prolifically and comprehending his queerness.

Baldwin's first collection of essays, *Notes of a Native Son*, was published in 1955, and his bleak and unabashed portrait of segregated life in America remains a mainstay of cultural studies. The essays in *Notes*, like many he wrote throughout his literary career, draw parallels between the movements for African-American civil rights and for gay rights, and between the African-American and queer communities, particularly the internalised shame, racism and homophobia that were rife at the time (and which still remain an issue today).

A skilled (and witty) debater, Baldwin became a public persona and a prominent voice in the civil-rights movement. He was a friend and confidant to both Martin Luther King, Jr and Malcolm X; he debated often with the latter on the true value of peaceful protest. Baldwin's convictions are best captured in his own words: 'Maintaining calm in the face of vitriol demands a tremendous amount of power'.

Chaz Bono

Cher has given this world many gifts, none more valuable than her and Sonny Bono's son, Chaz Bono. Born in 1969 and named after that year's cinematic flop *Chastity*, in which Cher had her first leading role, Chaz's life has unfolded squarely in the public eye.

In a 1995 interview with the *Advocate*, identifying then as a woman, Bono addressed tabloid gossip and came out as a lesbian. He was immediately thrust into a position of prominence in the LGBTQ+ community. A two-book deal led to the publication of *Family Outing: A guide to the coming-out process for gays, lesbians, and their families* (1998) and his memoir *The End of Innocence* (2002), which outlines the death of his partner Joan Stephens. As a contributor to the *Advocate*, the former Entertainment Media Director for GLAAD, and a spokesperson for the Human Rights Campaign, Bono is a vocal advocate for the LGBTQ+ community.

When Bono transitioned in 2008, his celebrity status helped usher an awareness of the transgender experience into our cultural psyche. The intimate 2011 documentary *Becoming Chaz* screened at the Sundance Film Festival and, later, on the Oprah Winfrey Network. Bono remains in the public eye as a proud trans man.

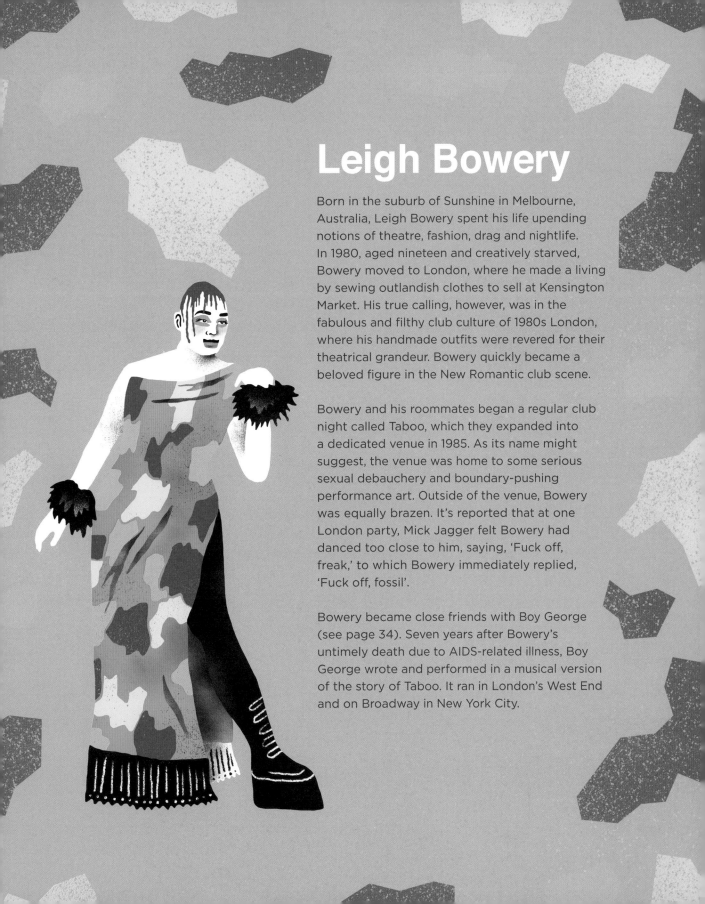

Leigh Bowery

Born in the suburb of Sunshine in Melbourne, Australia, Leigh Bowery spent his life upending notions of theatre, fashion, drag and nightlife. In 1980, aged nineteen and creatively starved, Bowery moved to London, where he made a living by sewing outlandish clothes to sell at Kensington Market. His true calling, however, was in the fabulous and filthy club culture of 1980s London, where his handmade outfits were revered for their theatrical grandeur. Bowery quickly became a beloved figure in the New Romantic club scene.

Bowery and his roommates began a regular club night called Taboo, which they expanded into a dedicated venue in 1985. As its name might suggest, the venue was home to some serious sexual debauchery and boundary-pushing performance art. Outside of the venue, Bowery was equally brazen. It's reported that at one London party, Mick Jagger felt Bowery had danced too close to him, saying, 'Fuck off, freak,' to which Bowery immediately replied, 'Fuck off, fossil'.

Bowery became close friends with Boy George (see page 34). Seven years after Bowery's untimely death due to AIDS-related illness, Boy George wrote and performed in a musical version of the story of Taboo. It ran in London's West End and on Broadway in New York City.

Judith Butler

Right now, we live in a moment where ideas about gender are discussed and reported upon constantly. Back in 1999, when Judith Butler's seminal book *Gender Trouble: Feminism and the subversion of identity* was published, gender was analysed solely on the fringes of academia. Butler's words (and vocal activism) have helped bring that conversation not only to mainstream academia, but also to mainstream society.

The key theory that Butler laid down in *Gender Trouble* is that gender is one big performance. For example: society only perceives that certain traits in men are masculine because we're stuck in a cultural feedback loop, repeating that same dance over and over, until it appears as fact. Binary ideas of how our gender should make us act or feel are involuntary, having been thrust upon on us as performance. (Mic drop.)

If that all sounds like something your gender-studies professor might say, you're probably right. Butler was the first to argue this point to such a wide audience, and after the publication of *Gender Trouble*, has continued to slay academically. Her contributions as a critical theorist have had a profound impact on feminist and queer theory, literary and film studies, and political philosophy.

Christine and the Queens

Hailing from Nantes, in the south of France, Christine and the Queens is the stage name of Héloïse Letissier, who now goes by an even simpler moniker: Chris.

Recording dream-pop bangers that are equal parts intriguing and catchy, Chris's unmistakable performance style is Michael Jackson-ian in its energy and theatricality. In interviews, Chris has repeatedly cited Jackson as her favourite male singer, and Patti Smith and Kate Bush as her two favourite female singers. A pleasant meeting of those three influences might be an accurate way to describe Chris's sound. While her debut record, *Chaleur Humaine* (2014), was melancholy, her second, *Chris* (2018), brought more of her stage presence and energy into the recording studio. Both albums have been gobbled up by critics and listeners alike.

It was between these two albums that Chris made the move to drop '-tine and the Queens' from her moniker, lean further into her androgyny and discuss her pansexuality in the media. 'In France, since I cut my hair, they hear the ambivalence in my lyrics way more,' Chris told the *Guardian* in 2018. 'I'm playing around with the male gaze and confusing heterosexual dudes.' Here's hoping for more colourful and confusing tunes from Chris, as soon as possible.

Laverne Cox

Known best as the inmate Sophia in the Netflix series *Orange Is the New Black*, Laverne Cox is a vocal trailblazer of the trans (and greater LGBTQ+) community. 'Sophia is written as a multi-dimensional character who the audience can really empathise with,' Cox said in 2013. 'They're empathising with a real trans person. And for trans folks out there, who need to see representations of people who are like them and of their experiences, that's when it becomes really important.'

In 2014, Cox appeared on Katie Couric's talk show, *Katie*, alongside fellow trans icon Carmen Carrera. The episode became infamous after Couric used cringe-inducing gendered language and repeatedly questioned both women about genital reconstruction. Cox deftly explained to Couric and her countless viewers how such objectifying language steered the conversation away from the lived experiences of trans women of colour, including the astronomically high rates of suicide and homicide they are subject to. It was pure poetry.

Cox is the first trans person to be on the cover of *Time* magazine and to be nominated for an Emmy Award in an acting category. Her 2014 MTV documentary *Laverne Cox Presents: The T Word* also scored her a Daytime Emmy Award for producing – just another trail blazed in Cox's burgeoning career.

Alan Cumming

Scottish-born triple threat Alan Cumming is as cheeky as he is talented. He's a rarity whose larger-than-life personality can either be cranked up or skilfully restrained – whichever the role necessitates. He's a chameleon of camp, and he's done it all.

Cumming's repertoire is wide-ranging, but often wanders into the realm of the tragicomic villain. He played Boris Ivanovich Grishenko, a henchman in James Bond film *GoldenEye* (1995); Fegan Floop, the deplorable baddie in the *Spy Kids* blockbuster franchise; and Loki, the god of mischief, in *Son of the Mask* (2005). Cumming has appeared in dozens of smash-hit Broadway productions, and scored a Tony Award for his portrayal of the Emcee in Sam Mendes's 1993 West End revival of *Cabaret*.

He has published a memoir, a photographic memoir and a full-length novel, and collaborated with his husband, illustrator Grant Shaffer, on a children's book. He owns (and lives around the corner from) Club Cumming in New York City, where he assists in curating its program of cabaret, and is also responsible for its strict 'no meanness' policy. While Club Cumming is up there, we must cast our minds back to 2005 in order to appreciate Cumming's greatest achievement in self-deprecating wordplay: the release of Cumming, the fragrance. That joke alone is worthy of a standing ovation.

ELLEN DEGENERES

In the 1980s, Ellen DeGeneres carved her own space in the male-dominated American stand-up circuit. Her endearing observational comedy style drew industry attention, earning DeGeneres the chance to perform on major late-night talk shows and a number of steady acting gigs.

In 1994, she landed the titular role in the ABC sitcom *Ellen*. During 'The Puppy Episode' in the show's fourth season, DeGeneres's character made history as the first main character in a sitcom to come out as a lesbian. The episode drew 42 million viewers worldwide and DeGeneres made the same announcement, this time out of character, on *The Oprah Winfrey Show*. Her honesty was rumoured to have peeved conservative executives from The Walt Disney Company, who owned ABC. In the fallout – which included criticisms that the show had become 'too gay' – *Ellen* was cancelled in its fifth season.

DeGeneres struggled to secure screen work, as she continued to polarise American audiences. After another unsuccessful sitcom (again self-titled), DeGeneres found her niche in the daytime talk-show format in 2003. Over its thousands of episodes to date, *The Ellen DeGeneres Show* has garnered critical acclaim, snatched dozens of Emmy Awards and secured a legion of loyal fans. DeGeneres has literally danced her way into the hearts and minds of America, all the while remaining a staunch advocate for the queer community.

In 2016, Ellen was awarded the Presidential Medal of Freedom by Barack Obama. An emotional Obama lauded DeGeneres's ability to 'make people laugh at some*thing*, rather than some*one* ... and to remind us that we have more in common than we realise.'

While hosting the 2014 Academy Awards, DeGeneres enlisted a troupe of Hollywood elites to join her in a selfie, with the objective of posting the most retweeted photo in history. She succeeded within two hours of tweeting the photo.

As the voice of Dory, the regal blue tang in Pixar's *Finding Nemo* (2003) and *Finding Dory* (2016), DeGeneres offered audiences of all ages the sage advice to 'just keep swimming'.

Asia Kate Dillon

Billions is an American TV series about the morally corrupt lives of venture capitalists and the efforts of those who seek to prosecute them. It's also the first American show to feature a major non-binary character: Taylor Mason, a hedge-fund analyst, played by Asia Kate Dillon, who identifies as non-binary. Dillon had previously found fame for their portrayal of white supremacist Brandy Epps in Netflix's *Orange Is the New Black.*

Contrasted with *Billions'* machismo world of high-stakes finance, the character of Taylor (who is a stock-trading prodigy) feels timely and refreshing, introducing into each episode the lived experience of those who live beyond gender binaries.

Dillon's *Billions* performance scored them a Critics' Choice Television Award nomination for Best Supporting Actor in a Drama Series, but awards season posed some issues due to the industry's adherence to the traditional gender divisions of actor and actress. When submitting their work in *Billions* for consideration for a supporting performance Emmy, Dillon first had to write to the Television Academy, pointing out the limitations of their binary award format. The Academy advised Dillon that they could submit to either the actress or actor category; they ultimately chose to enter the latter, because of the word's gender-neutrality.

Regardless of whether the entertainment industry chooses to address the gendered language of its award ceremonies, actress is a gendered term already on its way out of acceptable usage in the media. Performers are performers; actors are actors; and Asia Kate Dillon proves that you don't need to adhere to the gender binary to find critical success.

EZRA MILLER, lead wallflower in *The Perks of Being a Wallflower* (2012) and scary teen psychopath from *We Need to Talk About Kevin* (2011), is genderfluid.

TILDA SWINTON, androgynous star of the silver screen and Bowie doppelgänger, has said she that while she is 'probably a woman', she revels in the fluidity of her gender.

MILEY CYRUS, former Disney kid and uproarious superstar, cites her genderfluidity as a key part of her (very, very public) identity.

And now:

Gender Non-conforming Icons

A broader understanding of gender is slowly trickling down into the mainstream. This has been helped enormously by the increased visibility of gender non-conforming people in the public sphere.

GRIMES uses her large online following of pop-loving fans to discuss her own understanding of gender-neutrality.

JILL SOLOWAY, creator of the revolutionary TV show *Transparent*, is non-binary and gender non-conforming, and uses gender-neutral pronouns.

AMANDLA STENBERG, best known as Rue in mega-blockbuster franchise *The Hunger Games*, identifies as non-binary and pansexual.

Michael Dillon

Michael Dillon was born in 1915 to a rigidly aristocratic English family. Nearly forgotten by history, in the mid-1940s he would become the first trans man to undergo gender reassignment surgery, much to the delight of the tabloid media.

Dillon published his first book *Self: A study in ethics and endocrinology* in 1946, before the word transgender was even coined. 'Where the mind cannot be made to fit the body,' Dillon wrote, 'the body should be made to fit'. Throughout the book, Dillon kept private his own transgender experience.

It would be Dillon's aristocratic background that led to his outing as trans, with the 1958 edition of *Debrett's Peerage*, a publication covering the history and lineage of noble families in the UK, listing him as the heir to the title of his brother Robert, the eighth Baronet of Lismullen. A rival publication, *Burke's Peerage*, disputed this; its records mentioned only a sister (who would not be able to inherit the title). To avoid persecution, Dillon was forced to lie to the press, saying that he was born male but suffered from a congenital disorder of the urethra that required a number of surgeries to correct.

This was five years after Christine Jorgensen's transition (see page 50) became media fodder in the US. Facing a press storm of his own, Dillon fled all the way to the monasteries of India, where he spent the last four years of his life studying Buddhism and challenging fellow Theravada practitioners to allow a trans man to be fully ordained (he would eventually be ordained in the Tibetan branch of Buddhism). It was here he also penned his autobiography, *Out of the Ordinary*, which was published 50 years posthumously, in 2017.

Tom Ford

We live in the ultimate age of the slashie: there is no limit to the number of creative careers one might simultaneously have. And there are few slashies as accomplished (or stylish) as Thomas Carlyle Ford: Academy Award–nominated film director and producer *slash* visionary fashion designer *slash* business mogul.

In 1994, at the age of 33, Ford became the Creative Director of Gucci – and a household name. His vision was aggressively Americana – velvet hipsters and tight satin shirts – and helped yank the classic European brand into line with its contemporaries. In just two years, Gucci's sales would nearly double, saving the fashion house from near-bankruptcy. When Gucci acquired Yves Saint Laurent in 1999, Ford also assumed the role of Creative Director at YSL. In 2006, Ford launched his own eponymous fashion label. The likes of Beyoncé, Jennifer Lopez, Julianne Moore and Michelle Obama have all flaunted Tom Ford designs, while Daniel Craig wore his suits in the three most recent James Bond films.

Ford made his directorial debut in 2009, with a cinematic adaptation of Christopher Isherwood's classic queer novel *A Single Man* (1964). After focusing on fashion for the better part of a decade, he returned to the director's chair in 2016 with the thriller *Nocturnal Animals*. Both films are characterised by the kind of precise and chic production design you'd expect from Ford, a perfectionist in every arena.

JUDY GARLAND
Best pride (quasi-) banger:
'Over the Rainbow' (1939)

LADY GAGA
Best pride banger:
'Born This Way' (2011)

DIANA ROSS
Best pride banger:
'I'm Coming Out' (1980)

CHER
Best pride banger:
'Believe' (1998)

KYLIE
Best pride banger:
'Can't Get You Out
of My Head' (2000)

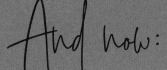

And now:

A Few Iconic Allies

Why were so many of our favourite queer anthems made famous by straight women? It might have something to do with a shared narrative. The entertainment industry (like most industries) has always treated women with contempt, and this was doubly true for women of colour. The allies listed here fought for their successes in the face of serious bullshit and adversity. These songs reflect a spirit of resilience to which the LGBTQ+ community can relate. Plus, they're just stone-cold bangers.

Jodie Foster

Challenging the stereotype of child star careening off the rails, Jodie Foster has graced our screens for almost her entire life. Appearing in commercials since she was three, Foster had her breakthrough role at twelve, when Martin Scorsese cast her as Iris, an adolescent prostitute, in his 1976 classic *Taxi Driver*. For her prodigious performance she was nominated for the Academy Award for Best Supporting Actress. From there, Foster made the rare leap from child stardom to Hollywood longevity, and has starred in blockbusters including 1991's *Silence of the Lambs* (for which she received one of her two Academy Awards for Best Actress), *Panic Room* (2002), *Inside Man* (2006) and *Elysium* (2013).

Foster's college years at Yale were embroiled in a drama of Hollywoodesque proportions. She was stalked by John Hinckley, Jr, an obsessed *Taxi Driver* fan who wrote her countless letters and even enrolled in a writing class at Yale in order to be close to her, slipping messages into her dorm room. In 1981, Hinckley shot and wounded President Ronald Reagan, as well as a police officer, a Secret Service agent and the White House Press Secretary. He explained that the assassination attempt was a ploy to garner Foster's affection. Needless to say, it did not work.

Foster has always remained relatively private about her queerness, although she has two children with her former partner of fifteen years, Cydney Bernard. It was not until 2013 that she came out publicly, during her acceptance speech for the Cecil B. DeMille Award at the Golden Globes. 'I'm just going to put it out there,' Foster said. 'Loud and proud, right? And I'm going to need your support – I am single.'

Lydia Foy

In July 2015, the Republic of Ireland passed the Gender Recognition Act. This allows a person's gender to be legally recognised by self-declaration, without any medical documentation required. It was a landmark move for a traditionally conservative and Catholic country, and one made largely thanks to the efforts of trans activist Lydia Foy.

Foy is a retired dentist from County Kildare. She began her transition in the early 1990s, and soon found herself tangled in the endless red tape of bureaucracy – just one of many struggles faced by trans and gender non-conforming folk around the world. The Irish Registrar General repeatedly denied Foy's requests to amend her birth certificate to display the correct gender, marking the beginning of her twenty-year-long legal battle.

Foy's first court case against the Registrar General was lost in the High Court in 2002, a ruling she would challenge in 2005, in light of Ireland passing the European Convention on Human Rights Act in 2003. Foy's tenacity kept the case in the international media. Council of Europe Commissioner for Human Rights Thomas Hammarberg condemned the Irish government's repeated challenges to Foy, stating, 'There is no excuse for not immediately granting this community their full and unconditional human rights'. Thankfully, these rights are now entirely protected under Irish law.

Stephen Fry

The UK enjoys its fair share of eccentrics, and among the country's most beloved is Stephen Fry. Fry is a perpetual joker, a national icon of stage and screen whose sense of style is fancily flamboyant. Comedian, actor, author, game-show presenter: the man has done everything, including advocated for mental health (he has been diagnosed with bipolar disorder) and the LGBTQ+ community. He's even the voice of all seven of the *Harry Potter* audiobooks.

Fry has attributed his becoming more vocal about his sexuality and LGBTQ+ rights to the counsel of Elton John (see page 44) and John's husband David Furnish. Fry is open about his own struggles with repressed homophobia – even publicly discussing his self-imposed celibacy of seventeen years.

In the BBC documentary *Stephen Fry: Out There* (2013), Fry explored the plight of queer people around the world, including capital punishment, high homicide victimisation and gay conversion therapy. In 2013, Fry also wrote an open letter to Prime Minister David Cameron and the International Olympic Committee, urging a boycott of the 2014 Winter Olympic Games in Sochi, Russia, because of the country's persecution of its queer community.

Hannah Gadsby

Nanette is a 2017 comedy act by Australian legend of deadpan Hannah Gadsby, a beloved regular on the Australian comedy circuit who has been praised for her ability to harness the audience's discomfort for her own comedic use. She gained international recognition for Josh Thomas's (see page 99) TV series *Please Like Me*, in which she played Hannah, a hybrid character merging Thomas's writing with her own personal struggles with mental health.

Gadsby grew up in the Australian state of Tasmania, where homosexuality was illegal until 1997. The homophobia and related sexual violence that she experienced in her home state make up much of *Nanette*'s heart-wrenching story.

Winning Best Comedy Show at the Edinburgh Fringe Festival, and eventually appearing on Netflix as a comedy special, *Nanette* is a total anomaly. Gadsby spends the gripping performance deconstructing stand-up comedy as a medium and forcing audiences to face some harsh truths about living on society's margins.

Despite the premise of *Nanette* being Gadsby's retirement from comedy, she has thankfully reneged on that promise. She has continued to perform, using her new-found international fame to champion queer voices with dignity.

ROXANE GAY

A brilliant provocateur and a rare voice of reason on Twitter, Dr Roxane Gay is a writer, editor, academic and survivor of sexual assault. Gay has addressed her experiences of rape at the age of twelve in much of her written work, and frequently pushes conversations about sexual violence into the public arena. Although her work is sometimes painful to read, it holds a much-needed mirror up to a society complicit in its own brutality.

In 2014, Gay's essay collection *Bad Feminist* catapulted her to the status of literary legend. Its essays are a masterclass in empathy and should be required reading for everyone. Her 2017 book *Hunger: A memoir of (my) body* is an emotional deep-dive into Gay's experience moving through the world as an obese person.

Above all, Gay discusses these topics in clear, simple language that all readers can grasp. Right now, that's really vital: these aren't lofty intellectual issues affecting solely the literary elite; bigotry and sexual violence are universal. In 2018, Gay edited *Not That Bad: Dispatches from rape culture*, an essay collection outlining the horrifying extent to which sexual violence dictates all of our lives. No doubt her voice will continue to be heard (and read) for a long time to come.

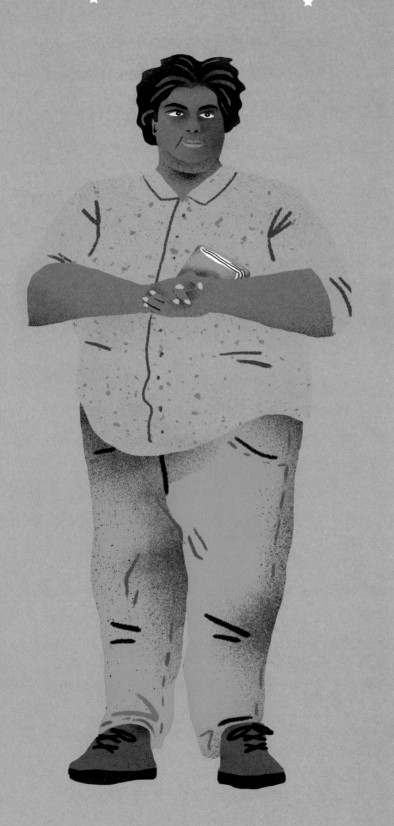

Gay began her undergraduate studies at Yale before ghosting family and friends to chase a romance in Arizona. Weathering a smorgasbord of struggle, Gay studied constantly throughout her life and received a PhD from Michigan Technological University in 2010.

The only pinned Tweet on @rgay's Twitter reads: 'It's fucking bullshit that Jack dies. There is plenty of room on that door. I am going to bed.'

Along with poet and academic Yona Harvey, Gay writes Marvel Comics' *Black Panther* spin-off series *World of Wakanda*. Harvey and Gay became the first women of colour to write a Marvel series and have been praised for their portrayal of LGBTQ+ characters throughout.

Boy George

Culture Club are legends of the English new wave music scene, known best for recording camp anthems 'Do You Really Want to Hurt Me', 'Time (Clock of the Heart)' and 'Karma Chameleon'. But it is their lead vocalist Boy George – DJ, singer, songwriter and fashion designer – who has always been the driving force behind the band's eclectic style. With his signature androgynous look and a persona that's visible from space, he brought an irreverent sensibility to their songs and live performances.

In the 1970s and 80s, during Culture Club's indisputable heyday, Boy George was heavily involved in London's New Romantic scene, a pop-culture movement characterised by glamorous, eccentric and historically inspired fashions. Since then, he has cycled through (and fused) glam, grunge and haute-couture aesthetics. (It's reported that his collection of iconic oversized bowler hats surpasses 300 in number.) Boy George was close friends with performance artist and avant-garde fashion icon Leigh Bowery (see page 15), and was the leading creative energy behind *Taboo*, a 2004 musical based on the eponymous debauched nightclub run by Bowery.

For a long time, Boy George was evasive about his sexuality. When questioned, he'd often simply respond by saying he preferred a 'nice cup of tea' to sex with anyone at all. By the mid-1990s, however, he had opened up about his secret relationship with Culture Club drummer Jon Moss, and in 2006 declared himself to be 'militantly gay' in the documentary *The Madness of Boy George*.

Gilbert & George

Partners in art and in love, Gilbert Prousch and George Passmore met in 1967 while studying at Saint Martin's School of Art in London. 'It was love at first sight,' George told the *Daily Telegraph* in 2002. Gilbert agreed: 'I followed like a dog'.

Rejecting the elitism and hyper-intellectualism of the art world, Gilbert & George's collective body of work has been made under one ideal: 'Art for All'. Much of their early work was performance art that saw them become living sculptures, while in recent decades they have focused on large-scale photography of pop-cultural symbols, often combined with self-portraiture and manipulated to resemble stained-glass windows.

The formal suits that Gilbert & George wear are something of a uniform; they are rarely seen in anything else. It's even rarer that the two are seen in public apart from one another: they are famously creatures of habit, eating breakfast together at the same cafe each day and taking the same route for their evening walk around East London. And while their performance art extends well beyond the confines of any gallery, Gilbert & George have exhibited at London's Tate Modern, the Guggenheim in New York City, the Museum of Old and New Art in Hobart, Australia, and as representatives of the UK in the 2005 Venice Biennale.

Masha Gessen

It takes nerves of steel to speak out against Russian President Vladimir Putin, especially from within the state he rules with an iron fist. Masha Gessen possesses these nerves, and as Russia's most recognisable LGBTQ+ activist – she once wrote that 'for years [she] was the only publicly out gay person' in the country – they have been put to the test more than once.

Gessen was born in Moscow, but as a teenager her family relocated to the US to escape anti-Semitic persecution. After the fall of the USSR in 1991, an adult Gessen returned to Russia, working tirelessly as a journalist in a nation state that doesn't enjoy the luxury of freedom of information and press. Her most famous critique of Putin came in a 2008 *Vanity Fair* profile, aptly titled 'Dead Soul', in which Gessen outlined the shady political dealings that secured his leadership.

In 2013, Gessen was assaulted outside the Russian parliament building, confirming her suspicion that she moved through her country under the threat of violence. For that reason, and fearing her son could be removed from her care, Gessen returned to the US. She continues to do stellar reporting (in both English and Russian) to expose the persecution of the queer community in her homeland.

Allen Ginsberg

Like much of the great literature from the Beat Generation, Allen Ginsberg's 1956 poem 'Howl' was conceived while tripping on peyote. Ginsberg spent much of 1954 and 1955 perfecting the three-part epic, which was revolutionary in its composition, each line reading as one huge breath. The final draft was an unmistakably anti-consumerist masterpiece.

In 1957, United States Customs Service and the San Francisco Police Department seized more than 500 copies of *Howl and Other Poems* as they arrived from a London printer. They branded the poetry collection as obscene, specifically the line which read: 'Who let themselves be fucked in the ass by saintly motorcyclists, and screamed with joy'. This sentence would become the focus of a highly publicised obscenity trial in the California State Superior Court.

Although sex between men was illegal in every US state at the time, Ginsberg made no attempts to conceal the parts of his own sex life reflected in *Howl*; he was unabashed in his queerness and confident in the literary value of a poem that had captured the attention of an entire nation. The judge ruled in favour of Ginsberg and his publisher, and the poem sealed Ginsberg's literary legacy.

Barbara Gittings

Formed in San Francisco in 1955 by Del Martin and Phyllis Lyon, the Daughters of Bilitis was the first lesbian civil-rights group in the US. In 1956, Barbara Gittings met Martin and Lyons, who, after seeing her spirited contribution to her first meeting of the DOB, asked Gittings to open the organisation's New York City chapter.

Gittings was the DOB's New York City chapter president for its first three years, and became instrumental in early civil-rights protests happening in New York City and around the country. In the 1960s, Gittings edited *The Ladder*, the official magazine of the DOB. It had a huge influence on its feminist and queer readership, and Gittings treated the publication like an apolitical queer think tank. She added the phrase 'A Lesbian Review' beneath *The Ladder*'s masthead, to make it clear what a bookshop browser might find inside.

Gittings' greatest legacy was her fight to end the classification of homosexuality as a mental illness. She and activist Frank Kameny battled the American Psychiatric Association to have homosexuality removed from the *Diagnostic and Statistical Manual of Mental Disorders*, a clinical tool that describes recognised mental illnesses. After much debate, Gittings and Kameny were successful in 1973. Gittings then committed her energies to forming the National Gay and Lesbian Task Force, working to combat discrimination through education and library programs.

Emma González

The 2018 Marjory Stoneman Douglas High School shooting in Parkland, Florida, resulted in the deaths of seventeen students and staff and injuries to seventeen others. And while the horrific actions of the shooter caught the attention of the public, it was the response from traumatised students that made waves in the media and the political sphere – waves that are still being felt today. Emma González, one of the survivors of the shooting, became an activist by circumstance and the inadvertent face of a new gun-control movement.

Three days after the massacre, González addressed a crowd in Fort Lauderdale, Florida, delivering what's now known as the 'We Call BS' speech. On behalf of her fellow students, González called bullshit on claims from politicians that gun-control measures couldn't save lives. She called bullshit on gun lobbyists' refrains that guns aren't actually dangerous. 'We call BS,' González shouted, 'that us kids don't know what we're talking about, that we're too young to understand how the government works'.

Just one month after her fiery speech, González and her fellow survivors organised the March for Our Lives, a series of rallies around the country that called for action on gun control. The crowd in the nation's capital was estimated to be as big as 800,000, making it the largest youth-led protest since those objecting to the Vietnam War.

KEITH HARING

The pop-art doodlings of Keith Haring are among the twentieth century's most recognisable artworks. He first gained popularity in the late 1970s with his graffiti murals in the New York City subway, using blank advertising panels as his canvas. Haring's rise to fame was meteoric, and he spent the 1980s in a feverish state of creative output. Among his most iconic characters are the Radiant Baby (a faceless figure on hands and knees), the Barking Dog, and his cartoon UFOs.

Much of Haring's art is centred around his queerness and the HIV/AIDS epidemic. Haring was openly gay and used his new-found fame as a commercial artist, as well as his prominence in the New York City queer scene, to advocate for safe sex. He worked with public campaigns to promote condom use and to encourage the queer community to speak up about their experiences with HIV and AIDS. His accessible, sometimes hilarious, cartoon style was able to address the subject of HIV/AIDS without the morbidity and fear that usually characterised such discussions.

Haring brought attention to the Silence=Death Project, creating a large silk-screen adaptation of the project's iconic poster, which criticised the Reagan Administration's refusal to discuss or act on the reality of the HIV/AIDS crisis. Haring was diagnosed with HIV in 1988 and died of AIDS-related complications in 1990.

Haring's upbringing in Pennsylvania was deeply Christian; he was raised in the United Church of God, and in his teens joined an evangelical Christian sect called the Jesus Movement. He took a great interest in his father's amateur cartoons, but would leave his family behind to spend his early adult years hitchhiking around the US and selling T-shirts featuring his own anti-Nixon design.

The Keith Haring Foundation, which Haring founded a year before his death, continues to fund many non-profit organisations that empower young artists and provide resources for people with HIV and AIDS.

A number of public murals by Keith Haring can still be found around the world: in Berlin, Germany; Pisa, Italy; inside the Museum of Contemporary Art in Antwerp, Belgium; on an unassuming street in Melbourne, Australia; and, obviously, dotted around the streets of New York City.

Neil Patrick Harris

Doogie Howser, M.D. aired from 1989 to 1993 and starred Neil Patrick Harris as a (strangely believable) teenage doctor. Since then, Harris has transitioned from child star to Hollywood (and Broadway) star with aplomb. A true triple threat, he splits his time between acting on stage and on screen. Harris also writes and produces, and has served as President of the Board of Directors of Hollywood's Magic Castle. Yes, he is a certified and celebrated magician.

It was the hit sitcom *How I Met Your Mother* that cemented Harris's celebrity status into the 2000s. In his role as Barney, Harris created a lovable caricature of the macho womaniser. The character's catchphrases and effortless charisma endeared him to audiences, and Harris used the show as a springboard into fun Hollywood roles and a strong career in Broadway. Harris hosted the Tony Awards four times, in 2009 and from 2011 to 2013, and was credited with boosting the ceremony's television ratings.

While *How I Met Your Mother*'s second series was airing in 2006, Harris dispelled tabloid rumours and publicly came out as gay, introducing the world to his partner, David Burtka. The two were married in 2014 and have twins (the unquestionable stars of the Harris-Burtka family's delightful Halloween portraits). In 2015, Neil Patrick Harris became the first openly queer man to host the Academy Awards.

Harry Hay

Founded by English-born activist Harry Hay, the Mattachine Society – named after a group of masked anti-monarch rebels from the annals of medieval French history – was one of the first LGBTQ+ rights organisations in the US. The Mattachine Society was formed in Los Angeles in 1950, while Hay was still married to his wife of thirteen years, Anita – the couple had adopted and raised two children together – but Hay felt the mission of his Mattachine Society as a 'total call', and left behind the life he had built.

As the Mattachine Society grew in numbers, Hay was forced to leave his beloved Communist Party, which at the time (in 1951) was openly anti-LGBTQ+. Openly queer and a (former) card-carrying communist, Hay was seen as an anarchist by conservative activists of the early American gay-rights movement. They felt his Marxist views, shared by many Mattachine Society members, further alienated queer people in the mainstream. Hay couldn't have cared less.

From the outset of Hay's civil-rights activism, he was anti-assimilation. He championed visibility, which helped shape the message of queer activism on the American West Coast. He would co-found the Los Angeles chapter of the Gay Liberation Front in 1969, and spent the latter half of his life fighting for the rights of Native Americans.

ELTON JOHN

Never has a performer so relished their time on stage – or done so in such heavily sequinned glory – as Sir Elton Hercules John. Along with longtime songwriting partner Bernie Taupin, John punctuated the 1970s with worldwide number-one hits like 'Saturday Night's Alright for Fighting', 'Rocket Man' and 'Goodbye Yellow Brick Road'.

John's stage presence is pure camp, from his oversized rhinestone sunglasses and glittery disco-ball waistcoats, to Daffy Duck couture at his iconic live concert in Central Park. John came out as bisexual in a 1976 interview with *Rolling Stone* and married German sound engineer Renate Blauel in 1984. The two divorced in 1988, and in another *Rolling Stone* profile in 1992, John comfortably identified as gay.

Since the early 1990s, John has relentlessly fundraised for HIV/AIDS research and awareness. Each annual Elton John AIDS Foundation Academy Awards Party raises millions of dollars while maintaining its reputation as the most raucous of all Oscars after-parties. In 1993, John began a relationship with Canadian-born filmmaker and advertising executive David Furnish. Although John was criticised in the 2000s for dismissing British demonstrations for same-sex marriage, he would become a staunch supporter and activist for the cause in the 2010s. He and Furnish were married in 2014.

John's fundraising for the Elton John AIDS Foundation and his tireless efforts to increase HIV/AIDS awareness and resources led to his being knighted by Queen Elizabeth II in 1998.

A close friend of Princess Diana, John worked with Bernie Taupin to rewrite the lyrics for 'Candle in the Wind' to pay tribute to her at her 1997 funeral in Westminster Abbey. Seen around the world, the gut-wrenching performance is the most famous of John's career.

Throughout his career, John's spending habits have been the stuff of legends. In eighteen months, between 1996 and 1997, he reportedly spent £293,000 (US$382,000) on flowers alone. Flowers.

And now: Some Flags We Fly

THE (ORIGINAL) PRIDE FLAG

Although the flags that define the rainbow aesthetic of pride parades have six stripes, the original designed by Gilbert Baker (see page 11) features eight. The pink stripe was removed because of a short supply of pink fabric in San Francisco in the late 1970s, while the original turquoise and indigo stripes were replaced by one of royal blue. When manufacturing flags on such a gargantuan scale, practicality helps.

TRANSGENDER PRIDE FLAG

The transgender pride flag was designed by Monica Helms in 1999 and revealed the following year in Phoenix, Arizona. 'The stripes at the top and bottom are light blue, the traditional colour for baby boys,' Helms explained. 'The stripes next to them are pink, the traditional colour for baby girls. The stripe in the middle is white, for those who are intersex, transitioning or consider themselves having a neutral or undefined gender.'

BISEXUAL PRIDE FLAG

The bi-angles, or bisexuality triangles, are a longstanding symbol of the bisexual community. In 1998, Michael Page used the intersecting triangles as inspiration for his bisexual pride flag. Page designed the flag using 40 per cent pink, to represent homosexuality; 20 per cent purple, to represent an overlap between homosexuality and heterosexuality; and 40 per cent blue, to represent heterosexuality.

INTERSEX FLAG

Created in 2013 by Intersex Human Rights Australia, which fights for the recognition of intersex people's bodily autonomy in public and in policy-making, the intersex flag features a purple circle. It symbolises a wholeness and one's right to be who and how they want to be. In 2018, New Zealand became the first country to fly the intersex flag outside of its parliament.

ASEXUAL FLAG

There remains lively academic debate as to whether asexuality is a sexual orientation, or simply a lack thereof. Either way, there is an increasing awareness and understanding of the asexual slice of the LGBTQ+ community. This flag uses black to represent asexuality, grey for grey-asexuality and demisexuality, white for non-asexual partners and allies, and purple for community.

GENDERQUEER PRIDE FLAG

Also called the non-binary flag, the genderqueer pride flag celebrates those of us who express their gender outside of society's prescribed masculine–feminine dogma. The lavender strip represents the concept of queerness; white represents agender identities; and green is for those who fall outside of gender binaries.

Marsha P Johnson

A true legend of New York City's queer, art and drag scenes, Marsha P Johnson was (and still is) an emblem of the American gay-rights movement. In Greenwich Village, she was affectionately known as the Mayor of Christopher Street. Johnson's middle initial, P, stood for 'pay it no mind'. As in: 'Are you a man or a woman?' To which Johnson would reply, 'Pay it no mind'.

Johnson was one of the first drag queens to frequent the Stonewall Inn in the 1960s, when the bar began to allow entry to women and drag queens. In the Stonewall Riots of 1969 (see opposite), Johnson is often credited as being one of the first patrons of the Inn to clap back at police brutality and fight, essentially igniting the uprising. In her own accounts of the evening, Johnson played down her actions inside the Stonewall Inn.

Along with Sylvia Rivera (see page 82), Johnson was drag mother to the Street Transvestite Action Revolutionaries (STAR) House, a collective that provided shelter to queer and trans kids, the majority of whom were people of colour; Rivera and Johnson paid the bills through sex work. Johnson spent her life being harassed by police and sexually assaulted by her sex-work clients, and she suffered from poor mental health. Despite her struggles, Johnson cared first and foremost about protecting the LGBTQ+ street kids of New York City.

And now:
A Note on Stonewall

In the early disco hours of 28 June 1969, police raided the Stonewall Inn in New York City and sparked an uprising. Three years prior, the bar had been purchased by the Genovese crime family to cater to queer clientele in Greenwich Village. Although Stonewall management were usually tipped off to the police's monthly raids, this one came unannounced and at a moment when there were more than 200 people inside. Many were drag queens, transgender people, male sex workers and homeless LGBTQ+ youth. That morning, rather than disperse at the request of police, evacuated Stonewall patrons gathered outside and decided to clap back.

The ensuing riot was reported to have involved hundreds of people. Witnessing the police brutality against other Stonewall patrons was the final straw for this marginalised cross-section of LGBTQ+ revellers. The bar itself was torn to shreds, with police and some of the people they had detained barricading themselves inside Stonewall and waiting until tactical police units arrived. It was wild. No one – the police least of all – expected the patrons of a queer bar to show resistance. But rioting continued into the second night, and well beyond.

In the year that followed the Stonewall Riots, grassroots movements demanding queer rights were catapulted into the mainstream media. In 1970, on the anniversary of the rioting, the first gay pride march descended on Greenwich Village. Each successive year, more pride marches would be held in cities around the US and around the world. Most international pride events continue to be held toward the end of June to commemorate the significance of that night at the Stonewall Inn.

Christine Jorgensen

Trans trailblazer Christine Jorgensen grew up on the rough streets of the Bronx in post–Great Depression New York City. Jorgensen was drafted into the United States Army at the age of nineteen, at the very end of the Second World War. She was honourably discharged and returned to New York City after a year of service, and shortly afterwards started hormone therapy to begin transitioning into a woman. Jorgensen then travelled to Copenhagen, Demark, to undergo gender reassignment surgery.

It's now pretty well known that an obsession with trans people's surgery is harmful, derailing conversations about the lived trans experience. But in 1953, upon Jorgensen's post-op return to New York City, she happily embraced the media's branding of her as the recipient of 'the world's first sex change'.

Jorgensen's widely publicised transition helped upend the world's understanding of biologically assigned sex and gender as a part of our identities. At a time when modern TV talk shows were in their infancy, she would appear on American screens in feminine glory to talk candidly about her experience. Best of all, Jorgensen had a sharp yet friendly wit. Her charming persona was the perfect antidote to an often nasty world, and helped the average punter empathise with her extraordinary journey through gender.

Frida Kahlo

Mexican folk artist Frida Kahlo is a cultural phenomenon. Famed for her unflinching self-portraits, Kahlo's paintings depicted her experience of gender, class and identity. Throughout her life, Kahlo was unrecognised and overlooked as simply the wife of artist Diego Rivera. More than twenty years after her death in 1954, art historians (and us mere mortals) would come to acknowledge her as an icon of the feminist and Mexican-American civil-rights movements.

Kahlo's life was marred by illness and tragedy. She contracted polio at the age of six and was bullied because of it; she was sexually assaulted by a school teacher; and at eighteen she was nearly killed when the bus she was riding on collided with a trolley car. The accident led to years of bed rest and as many as 35 corrective surgeries.

In those isolated years, Kahlo would use a custom easel to paint while lying down. She had a mirror placed on the ceiling above her bed to allow her to perfect the self-portraits that would secure her status as cultural icon. Kahlo painted herself endlessly, often in full male drag, and continuously rewrote the rules of gender and femininity. Openly bisexual, Kahlo had many affairs with women throughout her life, including with Josephine Baker (see page 12) and artist Georgia O'Keeffe.

kd lang

Canadian-born musician Kathryn Dawn Lang grabbed the world's attention with her performance at the closing ceremony of the 1988 Winter Olympic Games in Calgary. The following year, Lang and Roy Orbison would win a Grammy for their duet rendition of Orbison's crooning classic 'Crying'. Since that rapid rise to international fame, Lang has enjoyed a successful music career walking the line between country and pop.

In 1993, Lang was featured on the cover of *Vanity Fair* receiving a barber's shave from Cindy Crawford. In the accompanying interview, Lang explained her trepidation about coming out publicly and her fear that fans and artists in Nashville would ostracise her – something that, thankfully, did not happen. She has since collaborated with industry legends like Tony Bennett and Elton John (see page 44), and contributed to countless film soundtracks. Lang would even make a second Olympic appearance, giving a heart-wrenching performance of Leonard Cohen's 'Hallelujah' at the opening ceremony of the 2010 Winter Olympic Games in Vancouver.

Lang's suited-up look is immediately recognisable; the album cover of her 1997 record *Drag* featured her in, well, drag. Having spent her career ignoring any conventional idea of how a female singer should look or dress, Lang looks all the better for it.

Annie Leibovitz

For some celebrities and cultural icons, one specific photograph comes to mind when you hear their name; American photographer Annie Leibovitz is responsible for many such portraits. Leibovitz's visual style is immediately recognisable: she bathes subjects in soft lighting, and uses her photography to tell a story. Her work has changed the entire art form of commercial photography, particularly in the realm of magazine publishing.

Leibovitz started her career as a staff photographer for *Rolling Stone*. After only three years, she was promoted to the position of chief photographer and spent ten years redefining the magazine's look. She captured cover photos of John Lennon and Yoko Ono, Marvin Gaye, Diana Ross, OJ Simpson, Bob Dylan, Patti Smith – basically every culturally significant figure you can imagine. Leibovitz would go on to shoot for *Vanity Fair* and *Vogue*, and exhibit her work around the world. In 1991, she became the first woman to hold an exhibition at the National Portrait Gallery in Washington, DC.

Leibovitz was incredibly close to feminist legend Susan Sontag (see page 94) from the late 1980s to Sontag's death in 2004. The pair ignored tabloid speculation as to the nature of their relationship, but in recent years Leibovitz has (somewhat cryptically) confirmed that the two were lovers.

'Black, lesbian, mother, warrior, poet' were the exact words Audre Lorde used to describe herself, and they sum up her spirit pretty damn well. Lorde's poetry, for which she is best remembered, glows with the revolutionary anger of the civil-rights and anti-war movements. 'I have a duty,' Lorde said, 'to speak the truth as I see it and to share not just my triumphs, not just the things that felt good, but the pain, the intense, often unmitigated pain'.

Navigating the conservative world of white academia as a queer person of colour, Lorde spent her life fighting to be heard. The warrior strength to which she often alluded can be felt in her poetry and in her 1971 novel *Zami: A new spelling of my name*. The novel is considered to be the first of an entire genre of storytelling (which Lorde called 'biomythography') that weaves together strands of memoir, mythology and history. Much of *Zami* is made up of poetic portraits of the women in Lorde's life, from whom she forged her own understanding of womanhood.

Lorde was an early pioneer of what we now call intersectional feminism. Her written work and tireless activism grappled with issues of privilege and class in the context of a feminist movement defined by straight white women.

Audre Lorde

Jane Lynch

Making it big in TV comedy is tough. As a woman, it's even tougher. Now add being six feet tall, openly queer and 40 years old. That was Jane Lynch's Hollywood handicap when she was cast as the tracksuit-clad Sue Sylvester on Ryan Murphy's (see page 69) TV hit *Glee*. It was the big break Lynch deserved after spending much of her career on the verge of visibility.

Lynch's early years in comedy were based in Chicago, where she was one of the first women to tour with The Second City comedy troupe – career springboard for entertainment royalty like Bill Murray, Dan Aykroyd, Steve Carell, Tina Fey and Amy Poehler. In 1980, Lynch moved to New York City, diving headfirst into the piano-bar scene – a magical world where showtunes and cocktails collide. She performed in comedy and cabaret, and began to openly date women for the first time.

After playing an inappropriate Smart Tech manager in Judd Apatow's *The 40-Year-Old Virgin* (2005), Lynch became a familiar face in mainstream comedy. She landed various voice-acting gigs and parts in *Role Models* (2008) and *Talladega Nights* (2006) before performing alongside Meryl Streep in *Julie and Julia* (2009). She's currently the host of *Hollywood Game Night* and has picked up two Emmy Awards for her hosting prowess.

ROBERT MAPPLETHORPE

There's art designed to shock audiences just for the sake of it. Then there's art that uses shock tactics to turn the art world on its precious head. The photography of American artist Robert Mapplethorpe is certainly the latter. His striking images brought BDSM and homoerotic aesthetics into the mainstream art world.

Starting off with his prolific polaroid portraits, Mapplethorpe worked almost exclusively in black and white throughout his entire photography career. He possessed a natural flair for drama, understanding the power of lighting to create meaning. Mapplethorpe is known best for his graphic and phallocentric images examining kink culture, which approached the pornographic with the fastidiousness of high-art photography. A large part of Mapplethorpe's body of work is made up of highly formal and classic portraiture; he was also obsessed with still-life photography, having captured just about every variety of orchid and lily known to humankind.

Mapplethorpe was deeply embedded in the New York City art scene of the 1970s, rubbing shoulders with contemporaries like Andy Warhol and David Hockney, as well as iconic musicians like Iggy Pop, Grace Jones and Patti Smith (his longtime roommate, 'soulmate', lover and collaborator). Mapplethorpe died of AIDS-related complications in 1989, a year after establishing the Robert Mapplethorpe Foundation, which manages his estate and has raised millions of dollars for HIV/AIDS research and resources.

A book of Mapplethorpe's photography became the centre of heated debate at Birmingham City University in 1998. Local police confiscated the book from the university library, threatening to destroy the volume because of its sexually graphic imagery. The university prevented the book's destruction and any further police action, citing its rights to academic freedom.

Patti Smith chronicled her relationship with Mapplethorpe in her 2010 memoir, *Just Kids*. It's an awe-inspiring account of art-making, friendship, love and all the messy bits in between. Plus, the book's loaded with great insider stories from the art world of New York City in the 1960s and 1970s.

In 2017, a platinum print of Mapplethorpe's 1987 self-portrait sold for £450,000 (US$595,500), making it the most expensive photograph of his ever sold.

Tarell Alvin McCraney

The 2016 film *Moonlight* was a critical and commercial smash hit, winning the 2017 Academy Award for Best Picture (following a now-infamous envelope snafu) and becoming the first film with an entirely African-American cast to do so. It was also the first LGBTQ+ film to win Hollywood's highest honour. Director Barry Jenkins co-wrote *Moonlight* with Tarell Alvin McCraney, basing the story on McCraney's semi-autobiographical play *In Moonlight Black Boys Look Blue.*

In his writing, McCraney lays bare the bitter reality of growing up as a queer person of colour. Like that of *Moonlight*'s central character, Chiron, McCraney's childhood was spent navigating poverty, a parent with addiction issues and endless bullying. The film's story is bursting at the seams with McCraney's fear that he can never belong in any one social sphere, or to anyone at all.

In 2017, leading up to the Academy Awards ceremony, McCraney best explained his lived queer experience during an interview with the *Guardian*. 'My gayness doesn't give me any pass,' he said. 'I've still had the police pull me out of a car, put guns to my head, lock me in handcuffs and leave me face down in the pouring rain for no reason. Until they go into my back pocket and see some sort of white privilege in there, which is probably a university card or something and then they're like, "Oh maybe we've got the wrong person."'

Ian McKellen

Sir Ian McKellen has captured audiences' hearts on stage and screen, and is universally adored for his rascally personality. In the 1970s and 1980s, McKellen became a mainstay of the British theatre scene, performing regularly with the Royal Shakespeare Company and the Royal National Theatre before making waves in Hollywood. In 1991, McKellen was knighted by Queen Elizabeth II for his services to the performing arts.

Throughout his decorated film career, McKellen has played characters from all across the spectrum of dramatic energy. He perfectly epitomised wizardly wisdom as Gandalf in the *Lord of the Rings* trilogy, and glowed with evil menace as Magneto in the *X-Men* films. That being said, his greatest role has undoubtedly been as a constant champion of queer rights around the world.

McKellen came out publicly in 1988 to bring attention to Section 28 of the Local Government Bill, which was being considered by the British Parliament. This section demonised and endangered members of the LGBTQ+ community, particularly young people, by – among other things – associating homosexuality with predatory behaviour, shutting down support groups and preventing teachers from stepping in to stop homophobic bullying. Since fighting Section 28 throughout the 1990s and into the early 2000s, McKellen has continued to use his platform to raise international awareness for queer people facing persecution. He also co-founded Stonewall Equality Limited, the largest LGBTQ+ rights organisation in the UK and Europe, naming it after the Stonewall Riots (see page 49).

DeRay Mckesson

Black Lives Matter is a social-media movement that exploded in the wake of the inexplicable fatal shooting of seventeen-year-old Trayvon Martin and the 2013 acquittal of his shooter. Since that initial groundswell, BLM has continued to shine a harsh light on the experience of moving through public spaces as an African American, when violence and systemic racism can pose threats to one's life.

DeRay Mckesson is one of the most prominent voices of BLM, along with the three women who founded the movement and first spread its hashtag: Alicia Garza, Patrisse Cullors and Opal Tometi. Together, this group have harnessed the power of social media to raise awareness at a speed unmatched by few, if any, other movements in US history. In 2016, Mckesson and other key civil-rights activists were invited to the White House and spoke with President Barack Obama to discuss the state of race relations in the country.

Throughout Obama's presidency, Mckesson vocally held him to account for the platform of hope on which he ran for president. 'The landscape of hope is so different than it was in 2008,' Mckesson said of his meeting with Obama. 'Obama became a vessel of people's hope, and I think that will always be a set-up.'

Kate McKinnon

Oddball queen of improv comedy Kate McKinnon graduated from Ivy League Columbia University in 2006. The following year, she was cast on Logo TV's *The Big Gay Sketch Show*, appearing in all three of its hilarious seasons. McKinnon's deadpan delivery was so unique that she quickly drew attention from Lorne Michaels and the producers of *Saturday Night Live*.

McKinnon has appeared regularly on *SNL* since 2012, making her the longest-serving female cast member on the iconic sketch show. Her flawless impression of Hillary Clinton was just about the only enjoyable moment from the television coverage of the 2016 US presidential election. McKinnon is also beloved for her *SNL* impressions of Ellen DeGeneres (see page 20) and Justin Bieber. Her uncanny character work won her the Emmy Award for Outstanding Supporting Actress in a Comedy Series in both 2016 and 2017.

Now McKinnon is making strides into a career in Hollywood comedies: she was one quarter of the all-woman team in 2016's reboot of *Ghostbusters*, and also starred in *Rough Night* (2017), a film about a bachelorette party gone very wrong, as well as the underrated 2018 espionage comedy *The Spy Who Dumped Me*. McKinnon is carving out a space for herself on screens large and small, and we're excited to watch.

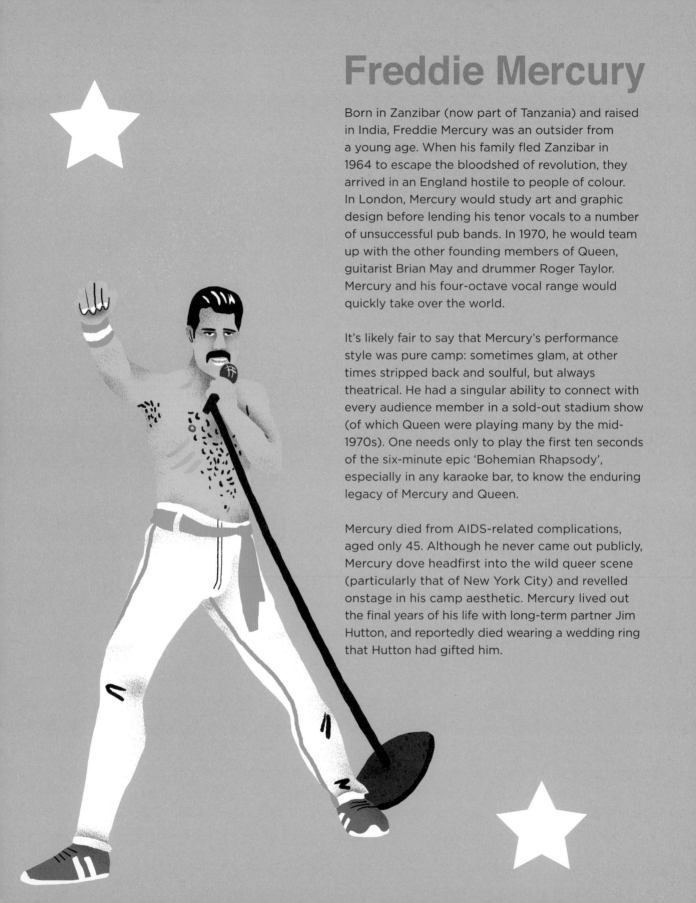

Freddie Mercury

Born in Zanzibar (now part of Tanzania) and raised in India, Freddie Mercury was an outsider from a young age. When his family fled Zanzibar in 1964 to escape the bloodshed of revolution, they arrived in an England hostile to people of colour. In London, Mercury would study art and graphic design before lending his tenor vocals to a number of unsuccessful pub bands. In 1970, he would team up with the other founding members of Queen, guitarist Brian May and drummer Roger Taylor. Mercury and his four-octave vocal range would quickly take over the world.

It's likely fair to say that Mercury's performance style was pure camp: sometimes glam, at other times stripped back and soulful, but always theatrical. He had a singular ability to connect with every audience member in a sold-out stadium show (of which Queen were playing many by the mid-1970s). One needs only to play the first ten seconds of the six-minute epic 'Bohemian Rhapsody', especially in any karaoke bar, to know the enduring legacy of Mercury and Queen.

Mercury died from AIDS-related complications, aged only 45. Although he never came out publicly, Mercury dove headfirst into the wild queer scene (particularly that of New York City) and revelled onstage in his camp aesthetic. Mercury lived out the final years of his life with long-term partner Jim Hutton, and reportedly died wearing a wedding ring that Hutton had gifted him.

George Michael

Listen to the first thirty seconds of 'Careless Whisper' and try not to sing along with saxophone-y noises of your own making. You can't; it's impossible. Along with 'Wake Me Up Before You Go-Go' and 'Don't Let the Sun Go Down on Me', this irresistible banger is only part of the legacy of George Michael. The English singer-songwriter dominated the pop charts of the 1980s and 1990s, first as the beaming face of Wham!, and then with a stellar solo career.

As well as being a beacon of LGBTQ+ visibility, Michael was a philanthropist of the most noble kind: anonymous. After his death on Christmas Day of 2016, charities came forward to report on his generosity. Michael reportedly paid for the IVF treatments of multiple women he'd seen discussing medical costs on various daytime TV programs. He's also said to have tipped a bartender £5000 after hearing about her student debts. The proceeds from a number of Michael's chart-topping singles, most notably (the lyrically problematic) 'Do They Know It's Christmas?', all go directly to humanitarian relief, and will do so in perpetuity.

Throughout his short life, media coverage of Michael's public persona was preoccupied with tales of substance abuse and court cases, but it's for these acts of kindness that he'll be remembered.

HARVEY MILK

Harvey Milk was closeted and civically indifferent until the age of 40, and the target of a political assassination by the time he was 48. In that eight-year interim, Milk uprooted a comfortable life in New York City to join the diaspora of queer men flocking to San Francisco's Castro District, where he would commit his life to local LGBTQ+ activism.

In 1973, Milk and then-partner Scott Smith were inspired to open a camera store after a local photo lab botched their roll of 35 mm film. As a business owner, Milk became increasingly frustrated with the rigmarole of the city's bureaucracy. He also witnessed the vilification of San Francisco's queer community at the hands of local police. Milk said of that time: 'I finally reached the point where I knew I had to become involved or shut up'. After years of campaigning and mobilising his Castro Street community, along with other large-scale LGBTQ+ rights groups, Milk was elected City Supervisor in 1977, becoming the first openly queer official to be elected in California.

Milk's first move as City Supervisor was to champion a civil-rights bill that outlawed discrimination on the basis of sexuality. He was also vocal about passing the 'pooper scooper law', which required pet owners to clean up any waste made in public – although he will likely be better remembered for his role as the self-proclaimed Mayor of Castro Street, and for his untimely death in 1978.

Milk's activism and assassination were portrayed in the 2008 Gus Van Sant–directed biopic *Milk,* in which he was played by Sean Penn. The film's production design team collaborated with San Francisco's GLBT Historical Society to flawlessly recreate the look and feel of 1970s Castro Street.

Although former City Supervisor Dan White assassinated Milk (and San Francisco Mayor George Moscone), he was only charged with voluntary manslaughter due to his 'diminished capacity' at the time of the murder. Local media then coined the term 'Twinkie defence', referencing White's consumption of junk food as a symptom of his depression. The term is now used to refer to a legal defence that is widely perceived to be bullshit.

In 2009, President Barack Obama posthumously awarded Milk the Presidential Medal of Freedom for his work to fight 'discrimination with visionary courage and conviction'.

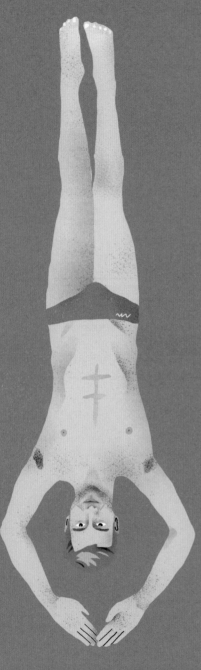

Matthew Mitcham

When he won a gold medal in the ten-metre platform at the 2008 Olympic Games in Beijing, diver Matthew Mitcham became the first openly queer athlete to become an Olympic champion. Born in Brisbane, Australia, Mitcham originally trained as a trampoline gymnast. He was scouted by the Australian Institute of Sport, who prompted his move to competitive diving.

In 2006, after years of training for and competing in international diving championships, Mitcham was burned out. He dropped out of the sport, suffering from depression, and supported himself with income from carnival feats: he would dive from a shocking height into a tiny barrel of water for the crowds gathered at the Sydney Royal Easter Show. After just six months, however, Mitcham began to crave competitive diving once more. He resumed training with new coach Salvador 'Chava' Sobrino to prepare for Beijing, where he would go on to make history.

After his 2008 victory, brand-new expectations compounded Mitcham's existing battle with anxiety. He became addicted to crystal meth and would fight to recover from his addiction in the lead-up to the 2012 Olympic Games in London. Since entering recovery and retiring from the all-consuming life of training, Mitcham has become a vocal advocate for mental health, addiction and queer visibility in the world of sports.

And now:

Visibility in Sports

In the 2016 Olympic Games in Rio de Janeiro, 41 openly LGBTQ+ athletes competed. Before that, in the 2012 Olympic Games in London, there were twenty-three openly LGBTQ+ athletes competing. This growth in numbers is indicative of the increasing visibility of queer sportspeople in a world that's traditionally (borderline painfully) heteronormative.

Babe Didrikson Zaharias is widely considered to be one of the greatest athletes of all time. She won two gold medals for track and field at the 1932 Olympic Games in Los Angeles, before swinging to professional golf – a sport she slayed by winning ten LPGA major championships throughout her career.

Caitlyn Jenner, divisive though she may be, is a trailblazer for the visibility of the trans community. Thirty years before appearing on the reality TV phenomenon *Keeping Up with the Kardashians*, she won a gold medal in the decathlon event at the 1976 Olympic Games in Montreal.

Jason Collins said in a 2013 *Sports Illustrated* article: 'I'm a 34-year-old NBA centre. I'm black. And I'm gay.' In doing so, he became the first man actively competing in a major American team sport to publicly come out. The move was a literal game changer.

Billie Jean King is one of the greatest tennis players of all time. She founded the Women's Tennis Association and fought for proper player compensation. In 2006, her legacy was celebrated when the USTA National Tennis Center in New York City was renamed the USTA Billie Jean King National Tennis Center.

In 2009, Gareth Thomas became the first active British rugby player to come out publicly as gay. The next year he was named by the *Independent on Sunday* as the country's most influential LGBTQ+ person. Years before that, in 1995, retired Australian International legend Ian Roberts was the first international rugby player to publicly discuss his LGBTQ+ identity.

Michael Sam made history in 2014 when he became the first openly gay football player to be drafted into the National Football League. President Barack Obama congratulated Sam, saying, 'From the playing field to the corporate boardroom, LGBT[Q+] Americans prove every day that you should be judged by what you do and not who you are'.

Janet Mock

Janet Mock is one of the most recognisable trans activists in the media today. While working as an editor for *People* magazine in 2011, Mock discussed her trans experience in a *Marie Claire* article titled 'I Was Born a Boy'. This became a springboard for her to get vocal about constant misgendering, which was evident in that article's title alone; Mock explained that such wording is problematic, because she has always been a girl. From there, in 2014, Mock released a memoir about her teen years in Hawaii, *Redefining Realness*. The book became a *New York Times* bestseller and opened many people's eyes to the lived experience of trans women of colour.

While on the promotional circuit for her book, Mock gained international attention for a contentious interview on *Piers Morgan Live*. She and Morgan's production team traded Twitter blows after the segment aired, with Mock explaining how the sensationalised framing of her life detracted from actual issues discussed in *Redefining Realness*.

Among a slew of contributor credits and LGBTQ+ activism commitments, Mock is also a writer, director and producer for the TV show *Pose*, which follows New York City's ball scene in the late 1980s. She is the first trans woman of colour to ever be hired as a TV writer.

Ryan Murphy

If you've watched TV in the last two decades, you know Ryan Murphy. The writer-director-producer is the brains behind *Nip/Tuck*, *Glee*, *American Horror Story*, *American Crime Story* and *Pose*. Murphy began his career as a journalist, writing for daily newspapers the *Miami Herald* and *Los Angeles Times*, as well as *Entertainment Weekly* magazine. He began screenwriting as a side hustle in the 1990s, and some of his show concepts stem from these early days in journalism.

Nip/Tuck was inspired by Murphy's undercover research for a story on the plastic surgeons of Beverly Hills. The medical drama scored him his first Emmy nomination, and ensured that the Fox Broadcasting Company would hire Murphy as executive producer and showrunner of *Glee*. The show garnered critical acclaim for its early seasons, which blended an exploration of many facets of the coming-of-age process – queerness, identity crises, self-doubt – with some irresistible pop covers. In 2011, a Fleetwood Mac–centric episode of *Glee*'s second season caused a resurgence in sales of the group's 1977 record *Rumours*, returning it to US and Australian pop charts.

Murphy's latest project, *Pose*, was inspired by Jennie Livingston's influential queer documentary *Paris Is Burning* (1990). Both revel in the glorious escapism of New York City's ball scene in the 1980s. Murphy donates all of his profits from *Pose* to the Sylvia Rivera Law Project and other organisations that provide resources to the LGBTQ+ community.

MARTINA NAVRATILOVA

Born in Prague, in what was then Czechoslovakia, Martina Navratilova was smacking tennis balls against a concrete wall at the age of four. By fifteen, she was national tennis champion, and three years later Navratilova had defected to the US to live and compete professionally. Throughout her stellar tennis career, she amassed a whopping total of eighteen Grand Slams, and 332 weeks ranked as world number one.

Navratilova was outed as queer in an interview with the *New York Daily News* in 1981, despite her request that the newspaper hold off on publishing anything until she was ready to come out publicly. In the eyes of the wider American public, Navratilova was queer, a communist defector, and unlike any notion of femininity with which they were familiar. Perhaps unsurprisingly, she suffered torrents of abuse from both within and outside of the tennis community. Meanwhile, Navratilova remained focused on her sport, inarguably dominating the world of women's tennis.

In 1992, Navratilova joined LGBTQ+ activists in a lawsuit that challenged the constitutionality of Colorado's Amendment 2, which removed protections for discriminating against queer people. She has also remained a vocal critic of communism, informed by her own experience growing up behind the Iron Curtain of the Soviet Union. Navratilova regained her Czech citizenship in 2009, thirty years after she fled to the US, and now lives as a dual Czech-American citizen.

'Aggressive' is one way that Navratilova's playing style was repeatedly described at the height of her career. Forever on the offensive, and unabashed about it when interviewed off-court, she redefined how women's tennis was played.

Navratilova's 1985 French Open defeat by longtime rival Chris Evert is considered by many to be one of the greatest tennis matches of all time.

In recent years, Navratilova has made headlines for a different reason: questioning the legitimacy of trans athletes in competition. In 2019, she penned an op-ed in London's *Sunday Times*, titled 'The rules on trans athletes reward cheats and punish the innocent', in which she used language for which she has subsequently apologised. Although her views are disheartening and almost certainly transphobic, we cannot diminish Navratilova's own efforts to increase queer visibility in the heteronormative world of sports.

Cynthia Nixon

Miranda Hobbes is one quarter of *Sex and the City*, HBO's iconic TV series that followed four women and their fabulous New York City lives. The witty and career-minded character of Miranda was made iconic by actor Cynthia Nixon, who used the role to launch her screen career. Most importantly, Nixon (a diehard Democrat) has used her considerable platform to champion LGBTQ+ rights and push for progressive political reform.

Nixon was diagnosed with breast cancer in 2006, but initially kept the news private for fear it might damage her career. In a 2008 interview with *Good Morning America*, she went public with her experience and has since remained a vocal advocate for breast-cancer awareness. Nixon's own cancer was discovered during a routine mammogram, and she campaigns for all women to seek regular check-ups.

In 2018, Nixon announced her intention to run for the Governor of New York. She won an endorsement (and a line on the ballot) from the Working Families Party, but lost her bid at the Democratic primary against incumbent Andrew Cuomo. After Nixon lost the primary, the Working Families Party withdrew their endorsement of her and backed the safe option of Cuomo (thereby preventing a serious Republican challenge at the polls). No doubt Nixon will continue her political efforts, particularly fighting for improvements to public education, her greatest passion.

Simon Nkoli

South Africa's most prominent LGBTQ+ activist of colour, Simon Tseko Nkoli, spent his life working to dismantle apartheid and campaigning for HIV/AIDS awareness. Nkoli was vocal about the relationship between his race and queerness. 'If you are black and gay in South Africa,' he once said, 'then it really is all the same closet ... Inside is darkness and oppression. Outside is freedom.'

In 1984, South African police tear-gassed a peaceful protest in the Sebokeng township. The police fired their weapons into the crowd, killing roughly twenty of the protestors. Nkoli survived, but he and other survivors were arrested three weeks later while attending the funerals of those who were killed. Nkoli spent nine months in prison before being formally charged with treason due to his links with the anti-apartheid organisation United Democratic Front. This charge carried with it the death penalty and resulted in a 420-day trial and appeal process, through which ultimately Nkoli and other high-profile UDF members were acquitted.

During those four years in prison, Nkoli sought the support of the Gay Association of South Africa, the largest LGBTQ+ rights group in South Africa. This predominantly white group refused to support him based on his race. This led to Nkoli founding the Gay and Lesbian Organization of Witwatersrand, or GLOW, an inclusive LGBTQ+ rights organisation, after his acquittal in 1988. He would go on to organise South Africa's first pride march in 1990.

Graham Norton

It's a rare skill to be able to balance a dirty joke alongside a poignant observation about the human condition. That is Graham Norton's gift as an interviewer and the key to this Irish larrikin's international success as a TV presenter, comedian, actor and author.

Norton was a rising star of British TV in the 1990s, appearing regularly on Channel 4 and Channel 5 on talk-show guest spots and occasionally as a game-show host. His early talk shows *So Graham Norton* and *V Graham Norton* endeared him to viewers, who came to expect each episode to be innuendo-laden and loaded with cheek. Norton was always an openly queer TV presenter but, more than that, he brought with him an unabashedly camp and flamboyant comedy aesthetic. Queer and crass – you either loved him or hated him (but really, it was always the former).

The Graham Norton Show – Norton's longest-running and most widely viewed late-night talk show – has been broadcast by the BBC since 2007. The show often winds up with an incredible ensemble of guests sharing the one couch – few more iconic perhaps than the meeting of June Brown, of *EastEnders* fame, and Lady Gaga. In the company of such celebrity, Norton is clearly comfortable and always able to rouse a hearty laugh.

Tig Notaro

'Hello, I have cancer! How are you?' These words, delivered deadpan, are the opening lines of the stand-up routine that catapulted Tig Notaro to cult comedy stardom. In 2012, a few days after receiving her diagnosis of cancer in both breasts, she took to the stage in Los Angeles' Club Largo and worked through the horrifying news the best way she knew how: by making people laugh.

Audio of the routine was recorded, and Louis CK (then at the height of his industry influence) persuaded Notaro to sell a half-hour clip through his website. It instantly went viral. The powerful set, and the year immediately following its first performance, was captured in the documentary *Tig*, which premiered to critical acclaim at the 2015 Sundance Film Festival. The intimate film reaffirms what we as an audience already knew: that Notaro is particularly resilient in the face of repeated trauma. Her life story was again portrayed in the semi-autobiographical Amazon series *One Mississippi*.

In 2017, Notaro was instrumental in bringing to light industry rumours about Louis CK's shocking sexual misconduct. Despite her own professional relationship with CK – he was an executive producer of *One Mississippi* – she was the first in the insular world of comedy to break her silence and help champion the voices of his victims.

Frank Ocean

Frank Ocean grew up in the birthplace of jazz – New Orleans, Louisiana – before relocating to Los Angeles in the wake of Hurricane Katrina. There he charmed his way into the music industry, which recognised his raw songwriting talent. He started his career as a ghostwriter, penning lyrics for pop giants including Justin Bieber, John Legend and Beyoncé. Ocean joined LA hip-hop collective Odd Future before signing his own contract with Def Jam Recordings, whose influence sent Ocean into the R&B stratosphere.

In July 2012, one month after releasing his debut album *Channel Orange* to critical and commercial success, Frank Ocean came out as bisexual in a Tumblr post. He recalled his experience of first love as being with a man and eloquently thanked him for the wild ride. Considering Ocean's platform as a rapper and R&B artist, his striving for visibility is especially important, as the rap world is particularly heteronormative and loaded with machismo. Ocean's dreamy sound and lyrical sincerity are beyond reproach, and inject some direly required diversity into the world of mainstream R&B.

Ocean independently released his long-awaited second album *Blonde* in 2016, and its lead single, 'Nikes', is certified platinum. On another note, Ocean is also one of the biggest figures in R&B to really commit to (and own) pastel-coloured hair.

MA RAINEY was often billed as the 'Mother of Blues', and for damn good reason. She began recording prolifically in 1923, and her 1928 ditty 'Prove It on Me' was a clear nod to her numerous love affairs with women.

JOBRIATH, whose performances mixed cosmic rock with performance art, was the first openly queer rock musician to be signed with a major record label. He died of AIDS-related complications in 1983 and was reportedly found beside his white piano.

And now:

Queers in Music

Besides the global icons that become fodder for blockbuster biopics – looking at you, Elton John (see page 44) and Freddie Mercury (see page 62) – there were plenty of queer influences in the music industry of the twentieth century.

SYLVESTER recorded the ultimate pride banger in 'You Make Me Feel (Mighty Real)'. When the song was released in 1978, Sylvester was already a legend of the disco scene in San Francisco and New York City, beloved for his androgynous stylings.

LITTLE RICHARD was kicked out of his family home aged fifteen because his father disapproved of what he perceived to be Little Richard's effeminate behaviour. Well, it was in part his camp performance style that made Little Richard an enduring legend of soul and funk.

DAVID BOWIE flirted with bisexuality throughout the height of his cocaine-y phase, but told *Rolling Stone* in 1983 that he 'was always a closet heterosexual'. However, we have Bowie to thank for much of the androgynous aesthetics in pop culture today.

ROB HALFORD, the frontperson of Judas Priest, came out in 1998 as gay. His mosh-pit antics and iconic motorcycle-chic helped define the heavy-metal scene as we know (or at the very least, stereotype) it now.

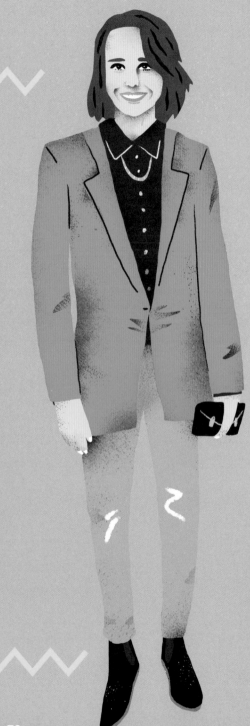

Ellen Page

Ellen Page found her breakout role in the 2007 indie hit *Juno*, Jason Reitman's coming-of-age comedy that dawned a new era of twee low-budget flicks. Although Page had already graced the TV screens of her native Canada, appearing in *Trailer Park Boys* and *ReGenesis*, and acted in Hollywood films like *Hard Candy* (2005) and *X-Men: The Last Stand* (2006), *Juno* shot her to instant fame and secured her a nomination for the Academy Award for Best Actress at the age of twenty.

From there, Page starred in the roller-derby classic *Whip It* (2009), blew our minds in Christopher Nolan's *Inception*, and reprised her role as Kitty Pryde in *X-Men: Days of Future Past* (2014). Alongside writer and curator Ian Daniel, Page hosts the Viceland documentary series *Gaycation*. Each episode of the show explores one culture from around the world and sheds light on what it's like to live there as an LGBTQ+ person.

Since the earliest days of the #MeToo movement, Page has been a vocal supporter. In 2017, she condemned Brett Ratner for allegedly outing her on the set of *X-Men: The Last Stand,* a decade before she publicly identified as queer. In 2019, Page slammed homophobic leaders around the world in an appearance on *The Late Show with Stephen Colbert*, which went viral. 'Connect the dots,' she implored. 'Kids are going to be abused, and they're going to kill themselves, and people are going to be beaten on the street … This needs to fucking stop.'

Sarah Paulson

As an actor on screen and stage, and with growing credits as a director and producer, Sarah Paulson has gone from strength to strength in the last two decades. With her power to flit between light-hearted comedy, gut-wrenching tension and tear-jerking drama, Paulson has an enviable dramatic range. Her multitude of cinematic supporting roles in film include *The Spirit* (2008), *Mud* (2012), *12 Years a Slave* (2013), *Carol* (2015), *The Post* (2017) and (perhaps less dramatically) *Oceans 8* (2018).

Paulson is best known for her recurring role on the FX anthology series *American Horror Story*. Paulson and co-star Evan Peters are the only actors to appear in every season of the show, playing a different character in each. It's tempting, however, to say that her greatest moments on the small screen are her recurring guest spots on *The Ellen DeGeneres Show*, where she is always the victim of DeGeneres's most savage pranks.

Paulson has openly discussed the fluidity of her sexuality when asked by the prying media. She has dated men and women, and had a long-term relationship with actress Cherry Jones in the 2000s. Since 2015, she has found a partner in American TV stalwart Holland Taylor. Although the pair originally met many years ago, they have both claimed that their new romance arose through private messaging on Twitter. Amazing.

Sally Ride

The sky is the limit for some. For American engineer and physicist Sally Ride, that proved not to be the case. Ride became the first American woman in space in 1983 and remains the youngest astronaut to have journeyed beyond our earthly atmosphere, having done so at the age of 32. While training for her mission on space shuttle *Challenger*, the media asked her many inane questions, including 'Will the flight affect your reproductive organs?' and 'Do you weep when things go wrong on the job?' To the latter, Ride coolly replied, 'How come nobody ever asks [mission pilot Rick Hauck] those questions?' Now there's a good question.

Ride was the only person to serve on the investigative committees for both the *Challenger* and *Columbia* space-shuttle disasters. It's reported that Ride was the first involved in the investigation to suspect that O-rings (basically, little rubber seals) malfunctioning at low temperatures could have caused the *Challenger* disaster (which they did). Ride spent her post-NASA career authoring books that encouraged kids to study outer space and the sciences.

Ride died of pancreatic cancer in 2012. Her obituary stated that Ride was survived by Tam O'Shaughnessy, her partner of twenty-seven years – a relationship that was, until then, kept private. This announcement added another historic element to Ride's 1983 space flight, with Ride being the first LGBTQ+ astronaut.

Adam Rippon

Following the skilled footwork of his mother
Kelly Rippon, Adam Rippon began ice skating
at the age of ten. In competitive skating years,
that's pretty late to the game. But he was a quick
learner, and began to dominate major youth
skating competitions around the US.

In 2018, Rippon would become the first openly
queer American skater to qualify for the Winter
Olympics. Winning bronze that same year in
Pyeongchang, South Korea, he became the first
openly queer American to receive an Olympic
medal. In the process, he won the hearts of
Americans – and of everyone else who tuned in
to the competition.

Rippon harnessed his new-found celebrity with
aplomb. In 2018, he won the twenty-sixth season
of TV reality competition *Dancing with the Stars*,
becoming the first openly queer winner in the
history of the series. Considering he won an
Olympic medal for essentially dancing on ice,
he might have had a slight head start on the
competition – but the achievement stands.

Later in 2018, Rippon announced his retirement
from competitive skating. We can only hope
that he will be clad in skin-tight clothing for his
next endeavour, whatever it may be. However,
it seems as though activism is more likely than
anything involving lycra. In an interview with
USA Today, Rippon criticised Vice President
Mike Pence for his apparent support of gay
conversion therapy. Rippon's comments gained
traction online, and forced the VP's press
secretary to finally address the allegations.

Sylvia Rivera

Born and raised in New York City, Sylvia Ray Rivera began to wear makeup in the fourth grade. Rivera's grandmother reproached her for her effeminate demeanour, and Rivera would end up living on the streets aged only eleven. Like many trans women of colour, Rivera used sex work to survive. She was eventually taken in by a tight-knit community of drag queens.

Like her close friend Marsha P Johnson (see page 48), Sylvia Rivera is a key figure in the Stonewall Riots of 1969 (see page 49). Although some (Johnson included) dispute whether Rivera was there for the first night of the rioting, her legacy is inextricably linked with that era of revolt against the New York Police Department. In 1970, Rivera co-founded the Street Transvestite Action Revolutionaries (or STAR) with Johnson, and worked to provide housing and resources for downtown Manhattan's homeless queer community and its many sex workers. STAR became a model for similar organisations in New York City and elsewhere in the US because of the effectiveness of its hyperlocal focus.

Rivera died in 2002 from complications related to liver cancer. That same year, trans civil-rights activist Dean Spade formed the Sylvia Rivera Law Project. The SRLP provides legal aid to people of colour who are trans, intersex or gender non-conforming.

Ruby Rose

In 2007, after a stint in the wild world of modelling, Ruby Rose won a nation-wide competition to become a music presenter on Australian MTV. She quickly became a familiar face in Australia, easily recognisable for her androgynous edge and (seemingly) effortless style. Rose was the face of MTV for four years before making the move into producing her own music and short films, the latter of which helped to hone her craft as an actor.

Rose gained the world's attention when she was cast as a recurring character in season three of Netflix's *Orange Is the New Black.* Rose played the inmate Stella Carlin, a cheeky love interest for the show's main character, Piper Chapman. When the season aired in 2015, Rose herself seemingly became the love interest of the internet at large. American audiences, like those in Australia nearly a decade earlier, were mesmerised. The role served as a powerful career springboard, with Rose taking fierce strides in Hollywood's direction – including nabbing the starring role in a new *Batwoman* TV series.

Openly queer since her early teens, Rose's framing of gender has received wide media coverage throughout her rise to fame. Although she prefers female pronouns, Rose is genderfluid, and says that her gender fluctuates from day to day.

RuPaul Charles is likely the most iconic drag queen of all time. Born and raised in San Diego, at the age of fifteen RuPaul moved to Atlanta, where he worked as a used-car salesperson to fund his self-described 'dragucation' – dancing in nightclubs and emceeing various events. He moved to New York City in 1984, where he became a habitué of the club scene. In 1989, he appeared in the B-52's video for 'Love Shack', which elevated his status from scene kid to star.

In the 1990s, RuPaul began recording dance and house tracks, including club anthem 'Supermodel (You Better Work)'. His growing profile as an artist clinched a spokesperson deal with M.A.C Cosmetics, making RuPaul the first drag queen to be the face of a cosmetics campaign. In 1996, he landed *The RuPaul Show* on VH1, where he interviewed major stars and lovingly channelled Oprah Winfrey, whom he cites as his biggest influence. RuPaul remained a major authority in the drag community, but it was with his production of Logo TV's 2009 cult reality hit *RuPaul's Drag Race* that he would become a pop-culture phenomenon.

Drag Race is currently in its eleventh season. Based loosely on the format of *America's Next Top Model,* the show pits drag queens against one another in a dramatic hunt for 'America's next drag superstar'. The show's power lies in its commitment to telling often-overlooked queer stories, showcasing incredible performers and throwing in some cheap laughs to keep us gagging for more. *Drag Race* has won RuPaul three Emmy Awards, and the show's (largely LGBTQ+) fanbase watch and revere the show as if it were gospel. Which, essentially, it is.

In his 1995 memoir, *Lettin' It All Hang Out*, RuPaul made clear his indifference for how he is gendered by others. 'You can call me he,' RuPaul wrote, 'You can call me she. You can call me Regis and Kathie Lee; I don't care! Just as long as you call me.'

Throughout *Drag Race*, RuPaul's relationship with the trans community has been strained by some of the language on the show – namely 'You've got she-mail!', a sound bite that formerly played in each episode. Then, in a 2018 interview with the *Guardian*, RuPaul made transphobic comments, questioning the legitimacy of trans women competing on his show. The backlash from contestants and their fans led RuPaul to apologise, and *Drag Race* now makes (rather pointed) efforts towards trans inclusivity.

RuPaul's favourite TV show is *Judge Judy*, and he discusses it often. He has earnestly described the reality show as his sanctuary, and said that its star, Judy Sheindlin, has helped him to better trust his instincts.

Bayard Rustin

As a civil-rights activist, Bayard Rustin will be remembered for many reasons. He was one of sixteen men who travelled the US by bus on the 1947 Journey of Reconciliation, which served as a model for the iconic Freedom Riders of 1961, and was instrumental in coordinating the March on Washington Movement. Rustin was a close friend of, and key advisor to, Martin Luther King, Jr. He urged King to preach nonviolence as an ethos of activism, something for which King is still celebrated today.

Throughout the 1960s and 1970s, civil rights were Rustin's primary calling. He was urged to keep his queerness private in his leadership role in the civil-rights movement, as it was feared it would negatively impact the publicity surrounding the cause. In the 1980s, he began to focus on LGBTQ+ activism, stating in a controversial 1986 speech that 'Gay people are the new barometer for social change ... The question of social change should be framed with the most vulnerable group in mind: gay people.' Problematic as parts of this sentiment might be, Rustin brushed upon the intersectionality of his queer identity: as a man who was both black and gay, he found himself pigeonholed in both of these communities.

When Rustin died of a burst appendix aged 75, he was on a humanitarian mission in Haiti. He was survived by Walter Naegle, his partner of ten years, whom Rustin had adopted when Naegle was thirty so that their union could be legalised – since marriage equality did not exist at the time. In 2013, Naegle would accept the Presidential Medal of Freedom posthumously awarded to Rustin for his civil-rights activism.

Tegan and Sara

Identical twin sisters Tegan Rain Quin and Sara Keirsten Quin are better known as the Canadian indie-pop band Tegan and Sara. They originally released music under the moniker Sara and Tegan, but realised that people mistook their name for that of a solo act: the non-existent singer Sarah Antegan. Tegan and Sara have released eight albums and are recognisable for their punkish style of streetwear.

Tegan and Sara have used their following to call attention to issues facing the LGBTQ+ and wider community. In 2012, they appeared on the cover of *Under the Radar* magazine's 'Protest Issue', with a sign declaring, 'The rights of the minority should never be subject to the whim of the majority'. Tegan and Sara were vocal throughout the campaign for marriage equality in the US, even creating an ice cream sandwich with Californian brand Coolhaus. The sandwich was double-chocolate cookie and salted caramel flavoured, and aptly named 'Til Death Do Us Part'.

In 2016, following the election of Donald Trump as President of the United States, the sisters founded the Tegan and Sara Foundation as a commitment to 'feminism and racial, social and gender justice'. The foundation raises awareness for LGBTQ+ girls and women, and works to fight for their visibility in a queer landscape where they are often overlooked.

David Sedaris

There is sass in the classic conversational sense, and then there is that literary brand of sassy wit. Of the latter, David Sedaris might be the greatest living master. Devout readers of his non-fiction (-ish) essays are familiar with the most intimate details of his life: family machinations and struggles, a passion for collecting litter on British highways, and the interior layout of his beach house (dubbed the Sea Section).

Many of Sedaris's collections are *New York Times* bestsellers, including *Naked* (1997), *Me Talk Pretty One Day* (2001) and *Dress Your Family in Corduroy and Denim* (2004). They're each the kind of book that will have you crying on one page and laughing maniacally to yourself on the next. Sedaris's sister – none other than Amy Sedaris of *Strangers with Candy* and *BoJack Horseman* fame – appears in many of the stories set in his childhood. The siblings frequently collaborate as writing partners, and were especially prolific in the 1990s, when they created absurd comedies to perform in New York City's Off-Broadway theatres.

Sedaris tours the world giving lively book readings, which are almost always sold-out affairs in large-scale venues. Afterwards, he's known to hang around and sign books for hours on end. The weirdest and most wonderful of his fan interactions are woven into Sedaris's most recent essay collections.

Alia Shawkat

As Maeby Fünke (pronounced *may-be feh-yoon-kay*) in Fox's cult sitcom *Arrested Development*, Alia Shawkat found her breakout role. Maeby was one of the show's only characters with even a shred of self-awareness, and Shawkat's savagely deadpan delivery was praised by critics from the outset. Between *Arrested Development*'s long hiatus from 2006 to 2013, Shawkat starred in Drew Barrymore's directorial debut, *Whip It* (2009), alongside Ellen Page (see page 78), and the pair remain close friends.

Since 2016, Shawkat has played the lead role in TBS's critically acclaimed dark comedy *Search Party*. It's a millennial whodunit of sorts, with Shawkat's neurotic and nuanced performance prompting much of the show's praise. In recent years, Shawkat has been increasingly candid about her bisexuality. In 2018, she co-wrote and starred in the eccentric comedy *Duck Butter*, a beautiful film about queerness, spontaneity and dependency.

In a now-infamous 2018 *New York Times* interview with the cast members of *Arrested Development*, Shawkat was the only person to vocalise the inexcusability of co-star Jeffrey Tambor's behaviour. Regarding his alleged outbursts of rage, other cast members spoke solely of forgiveness or remained silent entirely. Shawkat was clear, stating, 'That doesn't mean it's acceptable … Things are changing, and people need to respect each other differently.'

Jóhanna Sigurðardóttir

Jóhanna Sigurðardóttir was elected Prime Minister of Iceland in 2009, making history as the first openly queer leader of any country.

In 1960, Sigurðardóttir obtained a diploma from the Commercial College of Iceland and began working as a flight attendant for (the now-defunct) Icelandic Airlines. From those earliest years of her professional life, Sigurðardóttir was a part of the trade-union movement. It was these union links that would bring her into the political fold in 1978, when she was elected as a member of parliament representing the Social Democratic Party. Throughout a long career in the Icelandic parliament, she repeatedly vied for the top job in her political party. After losing her bid in 1994, Sigurðardóttir famously raised her fist and declared, 'My time will come'. Her assertion (in the original Icelandic) became a common turn of phrase around the country – and, clearly, Sigurðardóttir's time did come (albeit as leader of the Social Democratic Alliance).

Sigurðardóttir married Þorvaldur Steinar Jóhannesson in 1970, and together the couple raised two sons. In 1987, she divorced Jóhannesson, coming out as queer and entering a civil partnership with Jónína Leósdóttir, the novelist and playwright who would become the world's first 'lesbian first lady' (as she liked to call herself). On 26 June 2010, the day that marriage equality first came into effect in Iceland, Sigurðardóttir and Leósdóttir were married after their decades of partnership.

And now:
Leaders Around the World

In the writings and rewritings of history, there have been many reports of world leaders who were LGBTQ+. These include figures of ancient history (like Alexander the Great and Julius Caesar), to more contemporary history (including President Abraham Lincoln). Conjecture is fun and all, but today we have been fortunate enough to see openly LGBTQ+ politicians assume positions of global leadership.

2009–2013: Jóhanna Sigurðardóttir, Prime Minister of Iceland
Sigurðardóttir (see opposite) was the first openly LGBTQ+ leader in history.

2011–2014: Elio Di Rupo, Prime Minister of Belgium
Before becoming a member of the Socialist Party and rising through Belgium's political ranks, Di Rupo obtained a PhD in chemistry from the University of Mons. In 1996, a media scrum confronted Di Rupo about rumours of his sexuality. When one journalist asked if he was gay, Di Rupo simply responded, 'Yes – so what?'

2013–now: Xavier Battel, Prime Minister of Luxembourg
In the early 2000s, after years of academic rigour, Battel hosted *Sonndes em 8*, a talk show on the (now-defunct) T.TV network. This helped bolster his public persona in Luxembourg, of which he would become the Prime Minister in 2013. In 2015, the year marriage equality came into effect in Luxembourg, Battel married his partner, Gauthier Christian Destenay.

2017–now: Leo Varadkar, Taoiseach (Prime Minister) of the Republic of Ireland
Varadkar is not only the first openly LGBTQ+ leader of the Republic of Ireland, but also the first of Indian descent – and the youngest. Varadkar studied medicine and is qualified as a general practitioner. Varadkar's partner, Matthew Barrett, is also a doctor, and currently practises at Mater Misericordiae University Hospital.

2017–now: Ana Brnabić, Prime Minister of Serbia
Both Serbia's first openly LGBTQ+ leader and its first female leader, Brnabić has been working furiously to transform the international image of Serbia, with the aim to join the European Union by 2025. In 2019, when her partner, Milica Đurđić, gave birth, Brnabić became the first LGBTQ+ world leader to have a child while in office.

Troye Sivan

Like a number of celebrities today, Troye Sivan first gained popularity by vlogging on YouTube about everyday (some might say mundane) experiences – but we won't hold that against him. Born in South Africa, Sivan's family relocated to Perth, Australia, when he was two years old. Through his YouTube following and his singing performances in Perth, he piqued the interest of Universal Music in 2013, who plotted his path to pop stardom.

In 2015, Sivan released his first record, *Blue Neighbourhood*. But it was with the release of his second record, *Bloom*, in 2018, that he grabbed the world's attention with the raw sexual energy of his songwriting. The first song on the album, 'Seventeen', was reportedly inspired by a past Grindr hook-up, and its title track, 'Bloom', is an undeniable ode to queer love stories. Sivan's critical and commercial success proves that the heteronormative formula of pop music is not set entirely in stone.

Alongside his music career, Sivan has landed a number of acting roles. An almost unrecognisable Sivan portrayed a young Wolverine in the 2009 superhero film *X-Men Origins: Wolverine*. More recognisably – platinum-haired and all grown up – Sivan appeared alongside Lucas Hedges in the film *Boy Erased*, a 2018 drama based on Garrard Conley's explosive memoir about gay conversion therapy in the US.

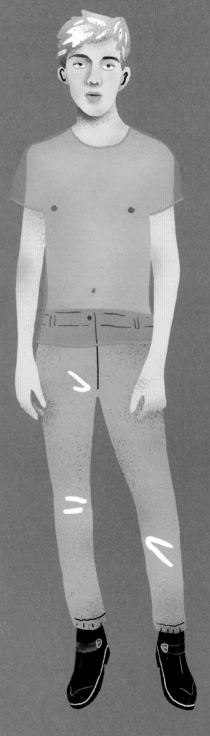

Stephen Sondheim

Stephen Sondheim has eight Tony Awards resting (presumably) atop his mantle – more than any other composer. They're (presumably) crammed in beside his eight Grammy Awards, his Pulitzer Prize for Drama, his Laurence Olivier Award and his Presidential Medal of Freedom. Sondheim's contribution to the world of musical theatre is hard to quantify, as his work has defined the medium as we now know it. Among his most well-known work, Sondheim wrote the lyrics for *West Side Story* (1957), and wrote and composed *Company* (1970), *Sweeney Todd* (1979) and *Into the Woods* (1986).

You don't need to be of the musical-theatre persuasion to appreciate a Sondheim composition. His lyrics are instantly recognisable for their complex wordplay and intense technical precision. Watching *Into the Woods*, should you (understandably) lose track of what specific story a song is spinning, its pointed structure will whack you right back on track. As a technician, Sondheim can manage this all while still being funny and clever, and bringing a dark edge to the sometimes frivolous medium of musical theatre.

Sondheim's work, whether or not it was ever his intention, has helped create a sanctuary for the myriad queer people who have discovered the world of theatre. For many in the LGBTQ+ community, the theatre was the first place that provided them a means of self-expression.

SUSAN SONTAG

Without question, Susan Sontag is one of the most influential thinkers of the twentieth century. Sontag wrote extensively about culture as she saw it, specifically human-rights atrocities, the HIV/AIDS epidemic, progressive political ideologies and the pitfalls of Western media. She also travelled to conflict zones – Vietnam during the war and Sarajevo during the Siege of Sarajevo – in order to observe and better understand such cataclysmic events.

Sontag's 'Notes on "Camp"', published in a 1964 issue of the *Partisan Review,* launched her literary and intellectual career. In the essay, Sontag defines elements of the camp aesthetic that underpin our culture. 'Camp taste has an affinity for certain arts rather than others,' Sontag wrote. 'Clothes, furniture, all the elements of visual décor, for instance, make up a large part of camp.' The theme of the 2019 Met Gala in New York City was 'Camp: Notes on Fashion', with the entire evening dedicated to Sontag's influential essay.

In her 1977 collection *On Photography,* Sontag dissected the proliferation of photography as both a craft and a hobby (decades before smartphone photography became a primary means of communication). She wrote: 'Using a camera appeases the anxiety which the work-driven feel about not working when they are on vacation and supposed to be having fun'. The next time you're at a crowded tourist destination, ready to scream at the next selfie stick that clunks you on the head, meditate on Sontag's observation – it might just soothe you.

From the late 1980s to Sontag's death in 2004, Sontag had a romantic relationship with photographer Annie Leibovitz (see page 53). Neither woman acknowledged their partnership publicly throughout Sontag's life, but Leibovitz did many years after Sontag's death.

Although famed for her non-fiction and critical writings, Sontag also penned a number of well-received works of fiction. Perhaps most important is her 1986 short story 'The Way We Live Now'. Told in experimental fragments of conversation, the story relays the fear and horror of the HIV/AIDS epidemic in New York City, when facts were scarce but many of the city's cultural elite were dying.

In her countless journals, Sontag would often write lists for the purpose of posterity. One such list reads: 'Things I like: fires, Venice, tequila, sunsets, babies, silent films, heights, coarse salt, top hats, large long-haired dogs, ship models, cinnamon, goose down quilts, pocket watches, the smell of newly mown grass, linen, Bach, Louis XIII furniture, sushi, microscopes, large rooms, boots, drinking water, maple sugar candy'.

Wanda Sykes

You might be surprised to learn that Wanda Sykes' first job after graduating from college was with the National Security Agency. Dissatisfied with her NSA gig as a 'contracting specialist', Sykes began her stand-up career by moonlighting at local venues in Washington, DC. In 1992, she quit the NSA and moved to New York City in order to pursue comedy full-time.

Sykes' first major accolade came in 1999, when she won an Emmy Award for her writing on *The Chris Rock Show* (where she was also a recurring guest). Sykes had a spate of film roles throughout the 2000s, including as a lead voice actor in *Over the Hedge* (2006). In her TV appearances, she often plays a thinly veiled version of her irreverent self – most notably, and savagely, in *Curb Your Enthusiasm*. In 2009, Sykes became the first LGBTQ+ person (and first African-American woman) to be the featured speaker at the White House Correspondents' Association dinner.

In 2018, Sykes was hired as the head writer of the tenth season of *Roseanne*, a revival of the popular ABC sitcom from the 1990s, which starred Roseanne Barr. Later that year, Barr tweeted a racist tweet, prompting Sykes to announce her immediate departure from the show. Sykes' decision likely caused ABC's quick move to cancel the reboot entirely (and eventually develop a spin-off, *The Conners*, sans Barr).

Magda Szubanski

Few Australian TV characters have a legacy as significant as that of netball-obsessed Sharon Strzelecki from iconic 2000s sitcom *Kath & Kim*. Strzelecki's absurd portrayal by comedian Magda Szubanski enshrined her in the hearts of all Australians (and those abroad lucky enough to catch the show). Szubanski has worked extensively in Australian film and television outside of her role as Strzelecki, both as a sketch performer and a screenwriter. But it's for her activism in the LGBTQ+ community that Szubanski has become an icon anew.

In 2017, the Australian Marriage Law Postal Survey was a political shitshow of the highest order. A government-funded survey was sent to every registered voter in the country, ostensibly to give parliament the best data on how we felt about marriage equality. Needless to say, it was a tumultuous time for LGBTQ+ Australians, who were made to feel like competitors in some nightmarish reality TV show.

Throughout the postal vote, Szubanski became one of the fiercest advocates for the 'Yes' campaign. Her appearance on *Q&A*, Australia's favourite political TV show, is regarded as a milestone of the campaign, as was her speech to the National Press Club, which she aptly titled 'What It Feels Like to Be an Unwilling Human Guinea Pig in a Political Experiment'.

George Takei

Best known for his role as Hikaru Sulu on *Star Trek: The Original Series*, George Takei appeared on US TV screens at a time when Asian-American representation was an unexplored frontier. Decades later, Takei remains in the public eye. This is partially due to his dad joke–laden Facebook page, which has a following of ten million people. But Takei is also a vocal advocate for the LGBTQ+ community and for broader human-rights issues.

Takei was born in Los Angeles in 1937. Shortly after Japan's attack on Pearl Harbor, Takei's family were forced into an internment camp in Rohwer, Arkansas. He was among the estimated 110,000–120,000 people of Japanese descent to be interned, most of whom were American citizens. Takei has focused much of his energy (and equity) into shedding light on this overlooked facet of US history. He's also a member of the Board of Trustees for Los Angeles' Japanese American National Museum, for which he has raised hundreds of thousands of dollars.

In 2017, speaking to a college auditorium in Dallas, Texas, Takei took aim at xenophobic policies enacted by newly inaugurated President Trump. 'Human rights are what makes us a civilised society,' Takei said, 'to recognise the humanity in each other. And that's very important, because sometimes, that fails us.'

Josh Thomas

In 2013, Australia's national broadcaster, the ABC, premiered *Please Like Me* on its youth-leaning channel ABC2. The show was written and created by its star, comedian Josh Thomas, who was already a familiar face on national comedy and talk-show circuits. The show's four-season run has become an unlikely cult hit, both in Australia and around the world.

Please Like Me is a semi-fictionalised account of Thomas's queer coming-of-age in Melbourne. Although his queerness is one of the show's central themes, *Please Like Me*'s wide appeal comes from its use of dark humour when tackling universal subject matter, such as mental health, the friendships of our twenties (when they're often the most important relationships in our lives) and love. Although *Please Like Me* is often likened to Lena Dunham's irreverent HBO show *Girls*, the two have very little in common, except that they're both shows about young people that were actually written by young people.

Since *Please Like Me*'s final episode in 2016, Thomas has been busy working on a new show called *Everything's Gonna Be Okay*, as well as posting photos of his dog John (a King Charles spaniel/poodle mix) on Instagram. John appeared in all four seasons of *Please Like Me*, playing himself.

Karl Heinrich Ulrichs

German writer Karl Heinrich Ulrichs was a trailblazer of the queer-rights movement. Born in 1825 in what was then the Kingdom of Hanover, Ulrichs worked as an advisor in the district court of the city of Hildesheim. In 1857, he was removed from his post when knowledge of his queerness became public. Five years later, Ulrichs would come out to his family and friends as Uranian (*Urning* in German), a term Ulrichs used to describe same-sex attracted men.

Ulrichs was the first to use the word Uranian, which is derived from the name of the Greek goddess Aphrodite Urania. Under the pseudonym Numa Numantius, Ulrichs began publishing essays about sexuality and gender. A few years later, in 1869, Austrian-born Hungarian writer Karl-Maria Kertbeny (who corresponded with Ulrichs often) coined the terms heterosexual and homosexual. Ulrichs himself refused the label of homosexual; as a scholar, he resented the hybridisation of the Greek *homos* ('same') and Latin *sexualis* ('sexual'). As a queer man, he detested the use of the word 'sexual', as he sought to separate his identity from constant reminders of sexual acts.

Towards the end of his life, Ulrichs would see other scholars begin to acknowledge and study queer identities. He wrote: 'I am proud that I found the courage to deal the initial blow to the hydra of public contempt'.

Jonathan Van Ness

When Netflix announced its reboot of *Queer Eye for the Straight Guy*, a collective groan rang out from the LGBTQ+ community. None of us foresaw that the newly minted *Queer Eye* would be so perfectly tender and so inclusive in scope. Nor could we have known that it would introduce the binge-watching masses to the new Fab Five's grooming expert, Jonathan Van Ness.

Van Ness grew up in Quincy, Illinois, a small city on the Mississippi River. Openly queer and unapologetically feminine, he was bullied mercilessly throughout high school, receiving repeated death threats from other students. It's through these horrible formative experiences that Van Ness began to nurture his ethos of self-love, which he advocates with sass and sincerity on *Queer Eye*.

Besides bringing us to tears repeatedly on *Queer Eye*, Van Ness works as a hairstylist in Los Angeles, and initially rose to fame for his absurd recaps of HBO's *Game of Thrones* in the *Funny or Die* web series *Gay of Thrones*. He also produces *Getting Curious with Jonathan Van Ness*, a weekly podcast that distils weighty subjects with the help of experts; in the episode 'Is Saudi Arabia Cute Now? with Prof. James Gelvin', for instance, Van Ness explores the issue of human rights in the Middle East.

Gore Vidal

American writer and public intellectual Gore Vidal possessed an unparalleled wit. His post-war novel *The City and the Pillar,* published in 1948, caused shockwaves in the world of literary criticism, as it defied the accepted narrative for queer characters – that they lived immoral lives, and usually died as a result. Vidal's satirical novel *Myra Breckinridge* (1968), written in the form of diary entries, is also considered a seminal text for its upending of social conventions of gender.

Vidal became a household name in America during the 1968 presidential campaign, when he took part in ten televised debates with conservative intellectual William F Buckley, Jr. The pair were pitted against one another because of their vast political differences, which were massaged by ABC network executives into quality TV. In the penultimate debate, Vidal famously accused Buckley of being a crypto-Nazi (a secret fascist). 'Now listen, you queer,' Buckley responded in fury. 'Stop calling me a crypto-Nazi or I'll sock you in your goddamn face, and you'll stay plastered.' Although commonplace in today's political discourse, at the time such theatrics during an ideological exchange were unheard of.

In the public eye and in his writings, Vidal refused to back down when challenged, and never capitulated when told how to live his life.

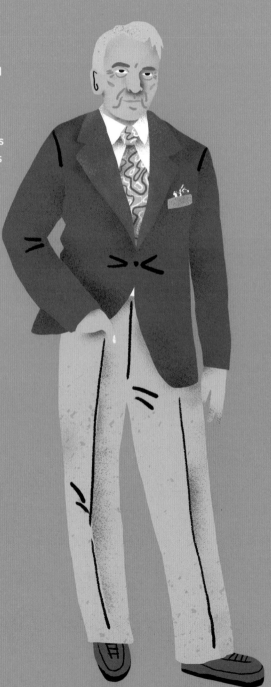

And now: Queer Literary Classics

Orlando **(1928)** Written by Virginia Woolf (see page 108), this novel is a fictional biography-of-sorts inspired by Woolf's lover Victoria Mary Sackville-West, Lady Nicolson. Orlando remains a classic in the canon of feminist and gender studies.

The City and the Pillar **(1946)** This work by Gore Vidal (see opposite) was the first major novel in which the protagonist is a gay man who doesn't die horribly.

The Price of Salt **(1952)** later republished as *Carol*, was the first lesbian novel with a happy ending. Because Patricia Highsmith was known as a successful writer of suspense novels, she first published this queer novel under the pseudonym Claire Morgan.

Giovanni's Room **(1956)** One of James Baldwin's (see page 13) few published works of fiction, this novel brought the notion of safe (and unsafe) queer spaces into the mainstream.

A Single Man **(1964)** Christopher Isherwood's novel beautifully captures unspoken queer partnerships and the nihilism of American students during the Cold War.

Rubyfruit Jungle **(1973)** Decades ahead of its time, Rita Mae Brown's novel is a heartfelt coming-of-age story about the lives of young queer women.

Holding the Man **(1995)** Timothy Conigrave's memoir might be the most revered LGBTQ+ book published by an Australian author. It's a heartbreaking account of love during the height of the HIV/AIDS epidemic.

Brokeback Mountain **(1997)** Long before the film, Annie Proulx's short story was published in the *New Yorker* to literary delight. It's a brief and perfect read.

Fun Home **(2006)** Before it became the Tony Award–winning musical, *Fun Home: A family tragicomic* was a graphic memoir by cartoonist Alison Bechdel.

A Little Life **(2015)** Hanya Yanagihara's 720-page tome was released to near-universal acclaim and became an obsession for readers who braved its wilfully traumatic storyline.

Lena Waithe

Some episodes of TV, through their artistry or sheer cultural significance, become standalone classics distinct from the shows of which they're a part. 'Thanksgiving', from the second season of Netflix's *Master of None*, is one such episode. It was co-written by Lena Waithe, who plays the character of Denise throughout the series, and the show's creator, Aziz Ansari. Before *Master of None,* Waithe was a staff writer on the police procedural drama *Bones*.

For 'Thanksgiving', Waithe drew upon her tumultuous experience of coming out – something to which many of its queer viewers can relate. As her character says in a flashback to her younger self: 'Being gay isn't something that black people love to talk about'. For her writing on the episode, Waithe won the Emmy Award for Outstanding Writing for a Comedy Series. Waithe was the first African-American woman to win the award.

'My mission is to make sure I'm not the last,' Waithe told *Variety* magazine. 'It's about making sure that other women of colour not only have a seat at the table, but that they're the best in the writer's room. It's not enough to have a seat at the table. You want to be so good that you sit at the head of it.'

Andy Warhol

Few artists require as little introduction as Andy Warhol. Prior to his days as prince of the pop-art movement, Warhol had a successful commercial career as an illustrator. He drew designs for women's shoes; illustrated book covers; and even made album covers for RCA Records. In the late 1950s, Warhol began exhibiting his artwork and quickly became an influential figure in the New York City art scene. His studio, The Factory, was a hotbed of pop art, a movement that sought to critique (or celebrate – critics disagree) American consumerism and redefine elitist notions of art. Warhol was also a faithful patron of the New York City club scene throughout his life, and The Factory was famed for its outrageous parties.

In 1968, Warhol was shot and nearly killed in an attempted murder by collaborator Valerie Solanas (who also wrote *SCUM Manifesto*). In his 1975 experimental memoir, *The Philosophy of Andy Warhol (From A to B & Back Again)*, Warhol wrote about the attack: 'Before I was shot, I always thought that I was more half-there than all-there … Ever since, I knew that I was watching television. The channels switch, but it's all television.' After the shooting, The Factory upped its security, which is said to have marked the end of its wildest era.

Warhol's many media include short film, screen printing, photography and painting. His highest valued work, *Silver Car Crash (Double Disaster),* sold for $105 million in 2013.

Irish poet and playwright Oscar Wilde is often said to be the most frequently quoted literary figure in history, beating out William Shakespeare and other wannabe wordsmiths. Many of Wilde's creative works, including *The Importance of Being Earnest* (1895) and his only novel, *The Picture of Dorian Gray* (1890), are considered among the most important in the English language. He was a master of harnessing dramatic effect to make comment on broad social and cultural themes. Wilde was persecuted throughout his life for being a queer man.

In 1895, Wilde attempted to privately prosecute Scottish nobleman John Douglas for libel. John Douglas was the ninth Marquess of Queensberry and the father of Wilde's lover, Lord Alfred Douglas, who was also known as Bosie. The Marquess had accused Wilde of committing sodomy (which was a crime at the time), and thus libelled his name. Wilde was forced to drop the libel case when the defence announced that they had male prostitutes willing to prove that the Marquess's claim was true. This judicial flop would be Wilde's downfall. A warrant was issued for his arrest for 'gross indecency'. Wilde was quickly tried and sentenced to two years of hard labour.

De Profundis (1905) was a letter Wilde wrote to Bosie during his imprisonment. The letter recounts their affair, and is a poignant meditation on Wilde's rapid fall from the graces of London's cultural elite. When Wilde was released from prison, he immediately fled to Paris. He would spend the last thirteen years of his life there in self-imposed exile, before dying of meningitis, penniless and only 46 years old.

The 'Alan Turing law', enacted in 2017, posthumously pardoned Wilde and an estimated 50,000 men who were cautioned or convicted under laws banning homosexuality. The law was named after English mathematician and father of modern computer science Alan Turing, who was convicted of 'gross indecency' for his relationship with another man. As punishment, he lost his career as a codebreaker with the government and was chemically castrated. He committed suicide a little more than two years later.

The Oscar Wilde Memorial Sculpture was commissioned by the Guinness Brewery to commemorate his literary legacy. Conceived by artist Danny Osborne, the sculpture comprises three statues in Dublin's Merrion Square. They depict Wilde, his pregnant wife Constance Lloyd, and a male torso representing Dionysus (the Greek god of drama, wine and fertility).

Wilde's final words were, reportedly, 'My wallpaper and I are fighting a duel to the death. One or other of us has got to go.' A true wit, even on his deathbed.

Virginia Woolf

Born into London's aristocracy in 1882, Virginia Woolf is one of the most influential writers of literary modernism – a movement that was part of the larger modernist philosophy, an intellectual revolution that sought to break cultural and social traditions. Woolf's writings, like those of her contemporaries James Joyce and Marcel Proust, are revered for being among the first to use stream of consciousness as a narrative device, where a narrator's internal monologue reflects the freewheeling ways in which human beings actually think and feel.

Some of Woolf's most iconic novels include *Mrs Dalloway* (1925), *To the Lighthouse* (1927) and *The Waves* (1931). Each are deeply experimental, bringing colour and texture to settings that could easily have felt hackneyed. Woolf was also an accomplished journalist and essayist. Her extended essay *A Room of One's Own* (1929), which was based on speeches she gave to university students, argued that women should demand literal and figurative space in which to write. In the literary and publishing worlds, where men dominated all conversation, it was revolutionary.

After her suicide in 1941, Woolf's literary profile waned. In the 1970s, as a scholarly focus on gender became popular, her work was retrospectively celebrated as decidedly feminist. *A Room of One's Own* and the follow-up novel–essay *Three Guineas* (1938) are still studied today for their sharp critique of patriarchal society.

Darren Young

Frederick Douglas Rosser III is better known by his ring name, Darren Young. In 2013, Young became the first WWE wrestler to publicly come out as queer while competing professionally, and has since spent his career as a vocal advocate for queer representation in that testosterone-loaded industry.

In the history of professional wrestling, queer stereotypes have been hurtfully satirised for entertainment (and box-office) value. During the sport's so-called First Golden Age in the 1940s and 1950s, Gorgeous George was one of the industry's brightest stars, strutting around the ring with a camp sensibility that scandalised American audiences (thus boosting viewership). In the 1980s, Adrian Adonis did the same, with a mocking flamboyancy that can only be described as cringeworthy. In this context, Young's effort to strive for visibility in wrestling is especially courageous.

In 2015, Young tweeted his anger about the WWE tour of Abu Dhabi, the capital of the United Arab Emirates. Young was furious about the organisation's decision to tour a country with a woeful record on human rights (particularly regarding its LGBTQ+ community). Young was not included in the tour's line-up, with the wrestling company stating: 'WWE cannot change cultures and laws around the world, and thus we did not send Fred Rosser to the United Arab Emirates for our upcoming events for his own protection'.

About the Author

Patrick Boyle is a writer and editor based in Melbourne, Australia. He contributes to pop-culture, arts, lifestyle, satire and queer publications. His most beloved icon featured in these pages is Elton John, whose camp ballads he has sung along to for over twenty years. This is Patrick's first book.

Thanks

I would like to take this moment to sincerely thank Paul McNally for the opportunity to write this celebratory book, as well as Rihana Ries for her editorial mastery in making my words sing. Thanks also to Alissa Dinallo, for stunning designs and vision.

And, while I have you here, I want to pay tribute to my mum, Tina Tasker. Although perhaps less well known than many of the people featured in this book, Tina is an icon of style in her own right. More importantly she's the most supportive ally any queer kid could ask for, and my best friend.

After creative stints in Strasbourg, London, New York City and Paris, Antoine Corbineau now lives and works in Nantes, France. Since Antoine's graduation from London's Camberwell College of Arts and the École Supérieure des Arts Décoratifs de Strasbourg, his designs have appeared in *The New York Times*, *The Guardian*, *Le Monde* and *Vanity Fair*, and he has collaborated with global brands like Apple, Google, Air France, Dior and Hermès.

Through a range of mediums and techniques, Antoine weaves a busy patchwork of texture and imagery. The end result is an energetic and unmistakable style. Antoine illustrated his first book, *Les Villes du Monde*, published by Editions Milan, in 2017.

About the Illustrator

PUBLISHED IN 2019 BY SMITH STREET BOOKS
MELBOURNE | AUSTRALIA
SMITHSTREETBOOKS.COM

ISBN: 978-1-925811-29-2

PUBLISHER: PAUL MCNALLY
EDITOR: RIHANA RIES
DESIGN & LAYOUT: ALISSA DINALLO
PROOFREADER: ARIANA KLEPAC

PRINTED & BOUND IN CHINA BY
C&C OFFSET PRINTING CO., LTD.

BOOK 106
10 9 8 7 6 5 4 3 2 1

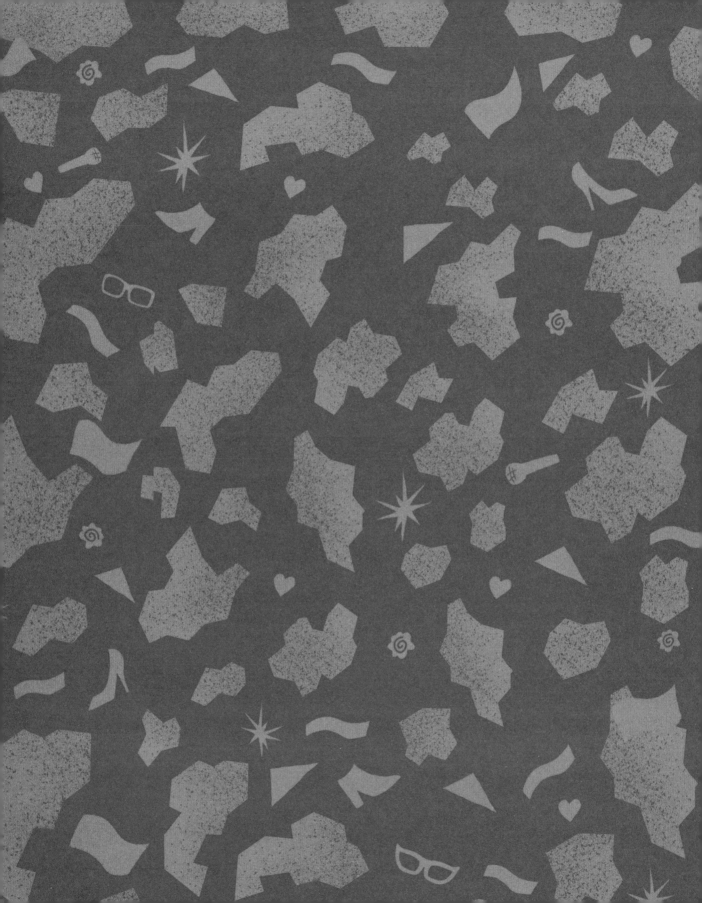